To Be Bc

CW00765176

Luce Irigaray

To Be Born

palgrave
macmillan

Luce Irigaray
Indepedent Scholar
Paris, France

ISBN 978-3-319-39221-9   ISBN 978-3-319-39222-6 (eBook)
DOI 10.1007/978-3-319-39222-6

Library of Congress Control Number: 2017931587

Cover illustration: © Christina Rahm Art / Alamy Stock Photo

Printed on acid-free paper

This Palgrave Macmillan imprint is published by Springer Nature
The registered company is Springer International Publishing AG
The registered company address is: Gewerbestrasse 11, 6330 Cham, Switzerland

Prologue: An Elusive Origin

Unveiling the mystery of our origin is probably the thing that most motivates our quests and plans. This question so much worries us that, perhaps, we have not yet begun to live, in ourselves and in the world. We would like to know from where we come, from what or from whom we exist, in order to dwell there and grow in continuation with that from what or from whom we are. Our most secret dream may consist in being a tree, the existence of which is determined by the place where it took root. Hence our ceaseless search for roots: in our genealogy, in the place where we were born, in our culture, our religion or our language, and also in what we project onto the most distant future but which, in reality, corresponds to the quest of the most indiscernible closeness. Who could maintain that they are not in search of their origin in their dreams regarding the future, their amorous desires, their longings for the beyond? Who has sufficiently thought about the nature of their origin so as to place themselves in relation to what or who they are here and now and be capable of making a decision only by themselves? In other words, who is able not to make up their mind according to a secret nostalgia for at least understanding in what their origin consists?

Now such grasping proves to be impossible. We become existent by cutting ourselves off—by ec-sisting—from our origin. Indeed, we were born as one from a union between two. We are the fruit of a copulative link between two different beings. Our own being is the incarnation which lives on of the conjunction between two human beings. Our existence is an actualization of the elusive event of a meeting between two humans—one masculine being and one feminine being—which gave birth to a boy or to a girl. We are for ever deprived of an origin of our own—we are neither a plant not God. We will always remain torn between the existence and the world that a vegetal being is capable of procuring for itself and the self-sufficiency, without beginning or end, of God. We are the ecstasis from a union, the unpredictable advent of a not appropriable event.

The origin of our being is in suspense in a connection between two terms which escapes any prediction and predication. And yet we are there—presence of an 'is' without any 'to be' that is originally identifiable. We are in charge of being—not to say of Being. We must take being into our care by preserving the power to be of the copulative link between two different humans, the place of a transcendence in relation to any personal existence.

We have not yet assumed such a destiny. We have not yet corresponded to our human fate. We imagine our lot in comparison with animality or divinity, but not as humans, the ones whose destiny is to take charge of their existence from a not appropriable essence.

Heidegger is not mistaken in saying that what we have imagined as humanism has not placed high enough the meaning of the humanity of man (cf. 'Letter on Humanism', in Basic Writings). Human destiny requires us to exist from an ec-sisting, that is, to ensure our being as ecstatic. Human being cannot develop from roots as a tree, or from an environment as an animal. Human being must take responsibility for existence beyond any continuity with regard to roots and background. And it is understandable that Heidegger wants Being to compensate for this lack of origin, when others resort to God, a mere natural immanence or a world built by man in various modes. However, human being only exists by taking on the not-being of a continuum—a break, a void, a nothing—with regard to its provenance and its environment. A human must give itself a being with faithfulness to the living that it is. In a way it must create its human being through relating to the world and the other(s)—be they plants, animals or humans—thus a being in relation which requires us not to be what they are while being able to be in relation to and with what they are, that is, capable of taking on the negative that the difference represents.

The way we become explains the interest that we take in our environment and our attempt to define the elements which have a share in it. But such a gesture is generally inspired by a desire to appropriate them and integrate them into a whole, rather than by an aptitude for not appropriating them, which the respect for the other as other involves. We have thus transformed the copulative process, from which we were born and are for ever exiled, into the general use of a copula—it is, there is—which decides on the existence of the real. We try to attribute to ourselves an origin by assigning an origin, a being, to everything and everyone that we approach, at a material or a spiritual level. But we do not correspond in this way to our human lot, a lot that requires us to be ecstatic in relation to our origin and our environment. Instead of endeavouring to perceive in everything and everyone their own being, we impose on them the not-being of a difference that we refuse to assume. We run the world in a sort of gallery of our projective embodiments, the only master of which is death.

If we assume our destiny as ecstatic regarding our origin, then we have no longer to project something of it onto the real. We can then be in a one-to-one relationship with any living being without reducing it to an object either of our judgement or of our desire or our love. No doubt that it is with humans who are different from us that such a way of being in relation is at once the most accomplished and the most risky. The ecstasis with respect to our origin leads us to wander outside ourselves and go stray from what allows a meeting between us to occur. We search for a possible mediation in a common world already existing, and yet it is the one which prevents us from discovering our own 'to be' and the path towards a possible conjunction with the other as other. Rather we must listen to the desire of the other which attracts us beyond a horizon defined by sameness and the already common, a desire which remembers the ecstasis from which we exist and calls us back to the question of our human being. And that for two reasons: it reminds us of our transcendence with regard to our origin and it indicates to us the transcendence of the other with regard to us. Only the consideration for these two transcendences, irreducible to one another, can give back to us a correct perception of the real, or of the being, of everyone and everything that we meet, especially of any being living by itself. And we will have to take into account too the transcendence of the world that we will form with the other. Assuming our human destiny will grant us aptitude for respecting the destiny of the other(s) and an enrichment due to their own being and existing.

Such a task seems superhuman; nevertheless, it corresponds to taking on our destiny. Is it not the one which allows us to leave behind the old man of the West for another conception of human being—towards finally attaining our humanity? How can we succeed in such an under-taking? First by cultivating our breathing, a resource that we too pas-sively left to the transcendence of a God extraneous to our terrestrial existence, whereas breathing is what permits us not only to live by ourselves but also to transcend a mere survival, to overcome the stage of a mere vitality so that we become able to achieve a human existence. Assuming and incarnating our sexuate belonging is the second element that renders us capable of fulfilling our natural existence while trans-cending it. This occurs thanks to a determination which provides us with a dynamism at once autonomous and relational able to transform our ecstatic fate into a personal incarnation that longs for sharing our ecstasies with the different other, which converts the abandonment of our birth into a solitude which gives us back to our being, but also to an original relation of desire and love with the other different from us by nature. It is through the rebirth, which this fundamental link grants us, that we can overcome the ecstatic character of our genealogical fate by consenting to the ecstasy of a union with a living being representing the other participant in our conception. In this deliberate ecstasy, we can take into our care that which means a donation of being, but also a withdrawal of being, in order to safeguard our specificity towards the achievement of our existence and its possible sharing. Thanks to what it grants us of life and access to transcendence, a cultivation of breathing allows us to assume the solitude of our singularity while venturing to share with another ontological destiny.

This requires courage, respect and care, but also the sunshine that love brings. According to the words of Phaedrus in the *Symposium* of Plato, Love, sometimes named Eros, has no parents, no age, no history, and its origin remains unknown to everyone. Love, whose destiny is said to be unique amongst the gods and humans, perhaps embodies desire for a conjunction always in search of its happening. Love would represent a dynamism longing for the copula incarnating the transcendence of our being. As such, Love would remain the everlasting yearning for the accomplishment of the ecstatic destiny of humanity.

However, we forget what a human destiny means, as we neglect how we can incarnate it. Hence, we wander in quest for a truth which could compensate for our lack of being. We attempt to justify and ensure this truth by the mastery of a copulative junction—now a logical one—which would guarantee the correctness of our judgements and predicative assertions. Through such a gesture, the most constant and somewhat authoritative in our cultural tradition, we inextricably cut ourselves off from the real, including that of our natural belonging, in the ecstasis of a discourse, of a logos. We create a being which proves being only 'smoke'—to quote Nietzsche—and that is already too much because we create above all nothingness. And it will be for ever so as long as we do not consider the two ecstasies from which we can exist as humans: the ecstasis with regard to our origin, and the ecstasis to which our desire calls us. These two different ecstasies, in a way these two not-being, must be taken on in order that we can discover what it means to be human and endeavour to incarnate our own destiny.

Contents

1

To Give Birth to Oneself

Whatever the unknown factors of our conception, we have wanted to be born. Our existence cannot be the outcome of a mere chance, and our will to live clearly manifested itself at the time of our birth. We were the ones who determined its moment. We were also the ones who gave birth to ourselves through our first breathing. In spite of the long dependence of the little human on others for its survival, it gave life to itself to come into the world, and it gave life to itself alone. Even if it has been conceived by two and it began its human existence in the body of an other, it is the one who, alone, decided to come into the universe of the living.

The true split between our will to live and our incapacity to assume this decision from the beginning explains most of the perplexities, difficulties, distresses and even suffering with which we will be confronted later in order to exist. It also determines many facets of our culture which seem to us as being pure creations of certain thinkers or artists, whereas they correspond to an attempt to convey the amazing enigma that the development of a human life means. The most striking expression of this enigma is the interpretation of our origin as the result of the breath that God blew into a matter made up of a mixture of earth and water. There is

© The Author(s) 2017
L. Irigaray, *To Be Born*, DOI 10.1007/978-3-319-39222-6_1

no question here of wondering about God himself, but about the fact that the will to exist, which our first breathing shows, is ascribed to God, the one who would be able to allow us to surmount the powerlessness due to our physical belonging. Another example, which contrasts with the first, would be the aptitude that some humans have displayed in undergoing hardships which seemed superhuman. Did they not find the capacity for doing that thanks to a return to the elemental will to live which allowed them to give birth to themselves?

Such a will to live at first acts naturally, independently of the intervention of our consciousness. Unfortunately our education does not teach us how to cultivate it at a conscious level. Rather we are taught to repress it under the pretext of adapting ourselves to norms which are supposedly necessary for a common existence, but which do not care a lot about our development as living beings. Instead of recognizing that life itself involves transcendence, and of teaching children to transcend themselves, thanks to a cultivation and a sharing of life, teachers more often than not require of them to forget life, to leave life at home—at best they permit children to express their vital energy in the playground—and to confine life as such at the level of needs. Amongst these are then relegated not only the need for taking shelter, for resting, for eating, but also a large part of our sensible or sensitive existence, of our sensory perceptions, of our sexuate belonging and of the preservation and cultivation of our breath. When this is not the case, these crucial aspects of our development become subjected to suprasensitive ideals, be they metaphysical or religious, without a real consideration for the necessity of their cultivation towards our individual growth, but also towards a coexistence with any other which would be truly human. Our way of educating does not take into account the child as a whole. In particular, bringing up the child scarcely respects the autonomy that it gained through breathing by itself and helps the child too little in the development of its potential towards a sharing of existence with other, human and not human, living beings. Our educative standards do not contribute to subjecting children to what or who they really are so that they can take charge of themselves and become who they really are by transcending and transforming themselves continuously. Indeed, being faithful to our own nature does not mean confining ourselves to that which our tradition calls our natural needs, but entails the cultivation of our natural belonging until its human achievement, including that of our relational attractions and our sublime aspirations.

If the little human succeeded in coming into the world by breathing by itself, a culture of its own breathing is also what can enable it to pass constantly from the vital to the spiritual stage of its existence. Taking charge of its breath and cultivating it is a means which can allow it to transcend itself here and now and to reach the beyond of a mere living state while being faithful to its earthly existence.

Such faithfulness requires each individual to correspond with a concrete finiteness through its sexuate belonging. The specificity of its sexuation is what acts as a finiteness inherent or immanent in nature which provides each with limits, measure and economy, including breathing—thus with a life of its own. The latter, then, loses its character of abstract universal, which remains extraneous to each particular individual and needs being incarnate.

By acknowledging and living itself as sexuate, a human being solves the question of its finiteness without necessarily having to resort to death. Its sexuate determination amounts to a structure which grants it the potential to internalize air—thus the breath, and the soul and even the spirit which were born of it—in a singular manner, at once concrete and particular, and which evades the sensible immediacy of a relation of nature to itself. Our sexuation supplies us with a setting—a *Gestell*, Heidegger perhaps would say—for the organization of the living, a frame which makes possible a return to, and a living within us, without going no further than an abstract and undifferentiated universality of life. Our sexuation represents a limited structure that life itself gives in order for us to develop according to our singularity. Our sexuate belonging does not imply that we experience only in an other the self-awareness that we have of ourselves—as we generally imagine and is even theorized by Hegel—but that we live ourselves as a being determined and limited. Which removes, from our experience of nature, its chaotic or abstractly universal aspect, to which only death or laws extraneous to life are able to bring a configuration or a shape.

Thus, there is no question of bending, from the very beginning, the child to an inescapable complementarity between two sexes which prevents it from developing its own sexuate potential, or of enclosing it in an unsurmountable particularity, but of making clear to it what is inscribed in its nature: this represents only one part of the whole humanity. As such a human destiny can be fulfilled: the newborn gives life to itself through breathing, and its sexuate belonging will act as a frame starting from which it can embody its own life.

The sexuate structure is not simply closed or open: it allows for a gathering with and within oneself but also for relating to and with the other(s). Without these alternations being mutually exclusive—as Hegel maintains, according to whom genus can be experienced only in an other, otherwise it might inhibit the circulation of the fluid or the motion of the process which ensures all the evolution of becoming— sexuate belonging can be neither merely experienced through an other nor achieved through performing copulation or reproduction; and it no longer has the vocation of bringing to a standstill the energy and motion of becoming into the particularity of one sexuate identity only either. This way of thinking underrates the value, at once energetic and structuring, of sexuation for the evolution of each human being. Belonging to a genus is what can ensure the passage from nature to culture, from singularity to universality. Our genus is the first parti-cular dwelling, the architecture or morphology of which opens up to meeting the other, others, and building a collective dwelling, a community of living beings.

Hegel himself admits that he has underestimated the importance of the genus in the dialectical process going from nature to spirit (cf., in Encyclopedia of Philosophical Sciences, § 366–370). The necessity for copulating and reproducing in order to render genus effective (cf., in Encyclopedia of Philosophical Sciences, pp. 369–70), or for sharing out the social qualities and roles in accordance with the genus (cf. *Phenomenology of Spirit*, Ch. VI), do not take into account the impact of the genus on the development of human life, on the constitution of self-awareness, on the desire by which each self-awareness is compelled to unite with another self-awareness in order to generate a spiritual world which remains faithful to nature. Sexuate belonging is both the place and the mediation which permit the passage of nature and spirit, the one into the other, in each individual, and in this way ensure a real link between one individual and another, between one individual and community.

Through its autonomous breathing and its sexuation, the little human gives birth to itself, it brings into the world a singular living being of which it will have to cultivate life, a life irreducible to any other, towards its achievement for itself and for the world into which it takes its place.

2

Coming into the World

Coming into the world initially means coming from an other, leaving a first environment, a first dwelling in an other. There the surroundings were liquid and warm, and the foetus lived in almost weightlessness, beyond the fact that its weight was carried by an other. Air and food were also provided by the other. Giving birth to itself, the new human behaves like a demiurge and takes an incredible risk. It can do nothing else, but such an exploit will prey on its entire existence as an incentive to and an anguish of venturing to attempt the impossible: to live by oneself. Coming into the world amounts to exposing oneself to dying for living.

Once we are born, we will always remember, even if we are not aware of it, that to live entails the risk of death. And this will always remain true, because living involves a perpetual becoming: if we do not become, we decline. But becoming requires us to venture beyond what is already experienced of life; and this does not happen without danger. Hence our ambiguous attitude with regard to our development: we waver between the refusal to grow and taking insane risks in order to exceed what we already are. This also explains why many cultures have transposed the permanent threat that the fact of living represents to a merely spiritual

© The Author(s) 2017

L. Irigaray, *To Be Born*, DOI 10.1007/978-3-319-39222-6_2

level which aims at living beyond death without facing the risk of dying here and now. At least it seems that this is so. However, is not Nietzsche right in maintaining that keeping our longings in abeyance thanks to suprasensitive ideals amounts to a sort of death? It would be possible, in this respect, to speak of a neurosis of our cultures which invite us to develop in a manner that only partly corresponds to our potentialities (cf. on this subject Paul Tillich, *The Courage to Be*, chapter 3).

By coming into the world, the newborn runs a total risk; but it is its life that takes this risk and not some plan that is more or less artificial and abstract with respect to life. The little being ventures into a completely changed environment with regard to its relation to oxygen, to food, to light, to gravitation and so on in order to get over a decisive stage of its becoming. In general it succeeds in achieving this exploit, which transforms our newborn into a sort of hero before whom everyone bows without understanding what they are saluting.

Alas, our young hero will be henceforth dependent on a world external to it for its survival. It is torn between omnipotence and helplessness, and it needs others to weave between these extremes. But others do not always value, or have often forgotten, the power of life itself, and they consider the newborn to be above all dependent on them to satisfy its needs and ensure its survival.

Few adults perceive the struggle, in a way the ontological struggle, which goes on within this little being: between the transcendental aspect of life and its inescapable empirical requirements; between air which is now the atmosphere in which the body is and the air it must breathe, and which is both internal and external to it, thus not favouring the perception of its own limits; between who it, itself, is and who others are: those who sometimes come into it through food, but also move it in space and give rhythm to its time, these others without whom it could not be, even though it already is. They are further questions which agitate it about the world that surrounds it and within which others move and carry it, a world in which sometimes it is daylight and sometimes darkness, that feels warm or cold, that is noisy or silent, scented or scentless, a world which both changes and remains the same. And all that does not yet take into account what happens inside it through breathing, digestion, the beating of its heart, the circulation of its blood, sleeping and awakening, motion and stillness, inside and outside. How could the newborn solve all these enigmas? In what order? How can they be linked together? All that is really difficult to imagine and so, like Zarathustra who is in search of a way of building a new world in the high mountains, the newborn sleeps a lot. While sleeping, sometimes it smiles as if it suddenly had discovered the solution of an enigma, or it is radiant with wisdom as a little Buddha; but, sometimes, it screams with distress too, perhaps because it meets with difficulty in being, and not merely because it is hungry or has stomach ache, as adults generally interpret its cries. They thus deprive it of its ontological belonging, reducing it to a universe of needs from which it has already freed itself by taking the risk of coming into the world.

However, adults worry little about helping it in the development of its breathing, the source of its autonomous life, at best confiding it to the vegetal world, a world which can help it without subjecting it. Indeed, as plants remain faithful to their own taking root this allows them to assimilate and transform better the elements which make them up—one of them being carbon 14. A vegetal environment can thus assist the newborn in assuming its life and entering a peaceful world which, furthermore, takes care of its more essential good: its breath.

Adults do not worry about reinforcing the baby in its sexuate belonging either, even if they were much concerned with and curious to know the sex of the foetus. Now sexuation is the structure which supports the unification of our being at a material and a spiritual levels. But if the newborn in a way has already all that it needs for being, it remains dependent on others for its needs, and this will maintain, for a long time, not to say for ever, a confusion between its immediate requirements and its potentialities. In order to realize the latter, it must win autonomy and a place of its own. It must free itself from the common space and time into which it entered, which are particularly represented by those who provide for its needs, and work out a place which suits its own way of inhabiting space and time. To this end, it is probably essential that it experiences its own potential for moving so as to discover the manner in which it can dwell. Unlike a tree, a human being does not at once live in the space and the time which suit it; it comes into the world by separating off from its first vital roots, and it is little by little that it will have to find, to elaborate and to construct a place which takes into account its natural potentialities and permits it to cultivate them towards a human blooming which corresponds to them. This place cannot confine itself to consciousness, as is too often the case in our Western tradition. It is from the body that it can be gradually shaped.

Quite lost, internally and externally, in the world where it is now, the newborn step by step undertakes its exploration through its perceptions. When it does not sleep, it listens to, tastes, smells, touches and begins looking at. Sensory perceptions mediate between it and the world, the world and itself. Its body thus acts as a mediator, and as such it cannot remain only passive. The body itself represents an agent of knowledge, but of a knowledge that we too often neglect, even forget, though this phase ought to be considered an important stage in the constitution of our being. Yet this phase does not obey the subject–object logic according to which we interpret most phenomena. Our baby has not yet a subjectivity strictly speaking, at least not a consciousness capable of clearly identifying the content of its perceptions and of integrating all it perceives into a whole.

Nevertheless, all that exists as sensations rather than as perceptions of determined things or objects with their own existences and qualities. For example, the newborn can perceive a colour, the sensation of which becomes inscribed in itself without its capacity for identifying to what or to whom this colour relates or to assigning a place to it in the global structuring of a consciousness. It has nevertheless perceived—Husserl would say 'apprehended', for example in *Logical Investigations* Chapter II—and it runs the risk of being overwhelmed with a set of sensations by which its body is driven without the capacity for analysing them, organizing them and freeing itself from them either. What will result from them in the future? Do our culture and, our education system, consider this first meeting between the newborn and the world with the seriousness that it requires, in particular its impact on the development of subjectivity? Do they take into account the anguish that the inflow of sensations to which it is unable to respond may arouse in the newborn?

Could not an aspect of our tradition be interpreted as an answer to this anguish: the fact of defining the world as a gathering of objects that we name, classify and integrate into a totality that we would be capable of mastering without being overwhelmed with many intense, contradictory, chaotic sensations which prevent us from constituting ourselves as a whole? And does not the beginning of Greek culture correspond to an attempt to pass from sensations, to which we are subjected, to an active and structuring perception of the universe? Could we not see in this a first stage in the constitution of our subjectivity, which bears witness to an effort of being situated in the world without cutting us off from our sensible perceptions? This stage would show the will, and even the courage, to assume our human destiny without isolating ourselves from the rest of the world by staying in a linguistic universe already structured and potentially closed, as will happen afterward. Hence a lack of cultivation of our physical properties, including with regard to their impact on our memory, which has handicapped our relational life, has gradually led to an exhaustion of our vitality and results today in a quite anarchical re-emergence of our natural belonging, of which we know almost nothing. What does Nietzsche teach us about the imprint of sensations on our body if not an almost explosive need for their expression, and also a necessary resort to art for supporting our becoming? And what did Freud comment on this subject if not the paralyzing effects of what we have lived without our knowing? Moreover, could we not observe a resurgence and a trying to approach phenomenologically these impacts in the work of Maurice Merleau-Ponty? And a refusal from Gilles Deleuze to repress them when he emphasizes the intensity of the sensations?

Unfortunately, all that does not yet help much the subjectivity of our newborn to develop by taking into account what it initially experienced. Furthermore, it will be asked to ignore, even to repress, what it has lived in order to adapt itself to the world into which it comes, without having really integrated and ordered—that is, without having made its own— the content of what it has experienced. Hence a desire, forever unappeased, to appropriate and even to take possession of all it will meet afterward. But such a way of behaving will above all cover again and render still more inaccessible what it tries to recover of itself.

3

Growing

Through its natural belonging, human being has in itself the source of the motion which leads it to grow. Its physical matter is endowed with an energy which urges it to develop, and not in an undifferentiated way, but in accordance with forms which are its own. Human being has the potential of a plant that grows by itself without needing an impulse brought to it from the outside. Nature, contrary to a fabricated object, moves by itself towards its blossoming. Of course, this 'by itself' does not exclude the intervention of other elements in its evolution. A tree grows by metabolizing the minerals on which it feeds through its earthly roots, thanks to the water of the rain, and the warmth and the light of the sun which reach it through the air in which they spread. The newborn also needs to metabolize the elements which lie in nature, but the fact that it does not take root in soil, as a tree, means that most of these elements must be brought to it, partly metabolized, in food form; hence it depends on people around it to obtain this food. Moreover, apart from breast milk, the food that will be given to it suits more or less its natural needs. We little by little discover what corresponds to the necessities of a human body and, more often than not, with cultural a priori which continue concealing its true nature from us.

© The Author(s) 2017
L. Irigaray, *To Be Born*, DOI 10.1007/978-3-319-39222-6_3

However that may be, the newborn has already in itself the motion of growth, as can be noticed through the changes in its appearance: it grows, it puts on weight, its expressions alter. To this process of growing up, the one of moving by itself in space is soon added. It begins with moving its arms, its legs, its hands and its feet, with their respective fingers. It has fun moving its body. And sometimes it is also upset about no longer knowing who or where it is amidst all these movements. Hence, it needs to grasp something solid: a part of its cradle, the body of the other, a toy and so on.

But the child wants to continue developing: it wants to live; and there is life only while there is growing one way or another. Thus, our baby attempts to sit up, tries to walk on all fours, before venturing to stand up, thus entering into a really human destiny. Standing up is a complex process that asks us to provide ourselves with a centre which contrasts with gravity. If digestion went on in a lower part of its body, the child must now raise its centring in order to acquire an equilibrium, for which its arms will act as a balancing pole at the time of its first steps. Gradually it must free itself from a centring that existed outside of itself, being in the one on whom it was dependent, in order to situate it in itself. It moves, crosswise, between forces of gravitation and forces of attraction, the former being more celestial and the latter more terrestrial. Its sensory perceptions and its longing for the other allow it to define little by little a horizontal path that it undertakes to clear. It begins living in a space of its own through its intention of making its way towards a place external to itself while overcoming subjection to gravity.

This really complex endeavour seems to go without saying for us Westerners, and if certain cultures, notably Eastern ones amongst which those of the yoga tradition, help us to cultivate the passage of the body from one position to another in relation to gravity, its situation in space, its sensory perceptions, especially the visual ones, instead our tradition does not care much about these sorts of questions, which are nevertheless crucial in order to discover a centring that takes place in the individual and allows it to reach a suitable constitution and autonomy. No doubt, such a centre in some way already exists in the child; if this were not the case it would not be capable of standing up and starting to walk. But this centring has not been considered seriously enough by our culture as an element crucial in structuring subjectivity. Instead of being really concerned with integrating the different stages of our becoming human, subjectivity has been constituted only from certain aspects: those capable of dominating natural growth through categories and principles which are imposed on it from the outside or from on high as modalities presumed suitable for human development. This means that the becoming of the little human becomes subjected to a purpose which substitutes itself for natural growth and blossoming, the source and motion of which lie in itself. It will be asked to submit its natural growth to meta-physical requirements already defined, the origin of which are not in its body: a thing that will paralyze its growth and tear it between a motion of which it is the source as living being and other movements to which it is subjected and which transform it into a sort of fabricated product, the mechanical functioning of which is dependent on an energy external to it, at least in part.

Because of its inability to provide for its needs from birth and its integration into a milieu which does not result from a cultivation of life, the child loses a part of its human potential, in particular the power of its natural belonging to transcend itself towards achieving its development, while remaining faithful to it and being capable of returning to itself, within itself, as a living being. The motion which has its origin in it and which develops by itself and also for itself as a living being weakens, disperses, gets lost in directions, forms, embodiments which do not conform to those of its nature. Hence, withdrawing into oneself, gathering oneself together, become impossible: two gestures which favour the creation of a place of one's own that is able to preserve the origin of the natural growing while granting a possible repose in oneself. Instead of continuing growing, blossoming and blooming in accordance with its nature, the development of the child is controlled and even structured by guardianships. Which means that various techniques, by substituting themselves for the motion of a natural growth, will paralyze and distort it, and transform human being into a sort of automaton in which a part, determined by culture, exerts control over another part, which remains faithful to nature, in order to master it while exploiting its energy. Using techniques— including those presupposed by our traditional logos—to which we ought to resort only occasionally and to support our natural evolution, ends in the latter's domination and its replacement. Then human being becomes a kind of manufactured product, whose accomplishment will be subjected to an idea—an *eidos*–of the human element which results from a culture instead of being a flowering of its natural belonging, notably into a fleshly face.

While its natural taking root is already problematic, the education that the child receives uproots it even more from its natural identity and terrestrial sojourn. This perhaps explains why it will seek in idealities how it can stand up and walk. Instead of finding within it a centre which helps it to negotiate with gravity, a celestial attraction will compensate for it and support the baby in its search of an equilibrium. Nevertheless, such attraction is partly artificial—even if human being is not indifferent to solar attraction—and jeopardizes the child as likely to be confronted at any moment with a void due to the lack of having placed a balancing pole, which counters terrestrial attraction, in itself. Perhaps the child has been asked to combine the motion of growing with the motion of moving in space without taking into consideration sufficiently the different intervention of gravity in both cases. Hence a lack, a nothingness, in its perception of itself and of the world, a nothingness with which it is unable to confront because it does not interpret its origin in a correct way. And growing will increase anguish with regard to this.

Thus growing, for a human being, no longer means becoming by oneself, a motion which characterizes the development of a living being, according to the still valid definition of Aristotle. Even if the newborn has in itself the source of its growth, its development will be inflected by models and behaviours which are ordered from the outside. A human being will never enter into presence according to a process determined only by its own energy. Its power to be present, its coming into a being present, are removed from it by the world into which it comes, a world in which natural growth must be bent to constructed imperatives that do not participate in the same energy. To be, for a human, will never amount to blossoming in accordance with its life or being present in its real achievement—one could say that it will never bloom according to its own face. When it is presumed that it has reached being a human, it no longer is, it has become a made product instead of developing into the one it is.

In reality, in order to grow the child would need a perpetual return to itself, but the way it is educated does not contribute to this. It would need to go back constantly to the source of its natural energy and to learn how to cultivate this as the mover of its becoming.

Such a motion of growing also requires an alternating with moments of repose in order to develop while preserving oneself. The gesture of gathering oneself together, of communing with oneself, which must go with becoming, can happen thanks to self-affection, a behaviour extraneous to our Western tradition, which practicing yoga and discovering cultures corresponding to this practice, as well as personal experiences, has allowed me to approach. Self-affection has nothing to do either with auto-eroticism or with narcissism, which are more familiar to us. Contemplating Buddha in meditation can lead us to glimpse what it is about. The matter consists of calmly staying in oneself, being silent, preferably with one's eyes closed, trying to perceive and concentrate in this way one's own inner energy. To succeed in this, I suggest focussing, at least in the first instance, one's attention on the perception of one's lips, one's hands and one's eyelids touching one another. Such a gesture—that I call 're-touch'—contributes to realizing what our limits are and the thresholds between the inside and the outside of the space that is ours, something which favours a repose in ourselves. It is possible to teach children how to practice self-affection in order to help them to develop, while remaining themselves, from their own energy and will so that they can ensure in this way an inner centring.

4

To Inhabit the World

The movements of the young child in space meet its delight at experiencing the power of moving and its desire to explore the world. This exploration begins with the mobility of its eyes, and it continues with the help of its hand which seizes elements of the surroundings so as to finger and place them near in order to observe them, often lifting them to its mouth, one of the first organs of investigation. The world of the child enlarges as soon as it can walk on all fours. Its energy seems inexhaustible and nothing can stop it in its discovery of the world. It would take incredible risks if adults did not repress its urges. At least it is the case in our culture in which warnings such as 'Pay attention, that burns!', 'You will fall down!', 'Do not touch that!' or 'Do not approach the edge!' often paralyse the gesture of the child. In other traditions—in India, for example—one allows the baby to have its experiences, considering them to be learning to live. It is true that if it burns itself, by coming too near to the fire, the child will be more prudent afterwards, whereas the repetition of a ban could awaken its wanting to check the validity of such a taboo or to experience things by itself, whatever happens.

In reality, our small child is mainly authorized to use sight in order to explore the world. It is unusual for it to be told 'Do not look at that!'.

© The Author(s) 2017
L. Irigaray, *To Be Born*, DOI 10.1007/978-3-319-39222-6_4

One seldom prevents it from looking at, although this could happen, in particular regarding erotic scenes. Now the relations that the child bears with its environment are not only dependent on the visible. It is possible that it may not favour this sense, except for satisfying other sensory appetites, for example touching, tasting and even listening to or smelling. To feel, with the sense of experiencing a sensation or a perception, is probably what inspires its tireless moving. And what it searches for is proximity, not to say intimacy, with the surroundings. Now sight is the sense of distance. Sight is the less physical and fleshly of our senses, at least in the way we are considering it, but also because of its neuronal constitution. If the child is curious about everything, this curiosity is still sensorial, carnal and not theoretical. And when Maurice Merleau-Ponty 'my translation' writes that 'a relation of principle and a kinship must exist between exploration and what it teaches me, between my movements and what I touch so that these are not only, like the pseudopods of an amoeba, vague and short-lived distortion of the bodily space but initiation and opening up to a tactile world', one may wonder whether he does not express a reminiscence of, even a nostalgia for, the first exploration of the world by the child he once was (cf. the chapter 'Interlacing and chiasmus' in *The Visible and the Invisible; my translation*). Amongst these experiences, in which touch has probably a major part, that of colour would act as a passage, the nature of which is above all tactile, between the external world and the inner world. What Merleau-Ponty experiences about colour recalls, in my opinion, the tactile and invisible passage of life from the outside to the inside of the body of which the child is in search and which represents its way of beginning to inhabit the world. No doubt, the baby still knows what it means to be living and does not yet situate itself within the circularity of a relation to the world in which the animate and the inanimate become confused. Certainly, living in a merely urban environment may lead to the fading of this difference for the child—but by projecting living onto things, rather than by reducing oneself to an object amongst those of the world, by becoming a thing amongst other things, as Merleau-Ponty would say. Which can happen afterwards, when the denominating will be substituted for sensible perception in meeting the real. In such a case, uniformity in the approach to the environment can make it miss the discovery of the diversity in relating to the world, especially regarding the distinction between the animate and the inanimate. This can even end in it forgetting the difference between what it perceives, when relating with a living being and with a thing, and in believing that approaching the former can occur only through eyes, be they in a way palpating as a hand—as Merleau-Ponty seems to think (cf. 'Interlacing and chiasmus' in *The Visible and the Invisible*). What he says on this subject looks to be a mixture of prenatal experience and confinement within a metaphysical horizon. His world amounts to the transposition of a placental dwelling without real exteriority and interiority. And if the importance that Merleau-Ponty attaches to sight does leave eyes with their discriminating potential it, nevertheless, seems to divert them from reaching a contemplative manner of looking at, which could give way to the tactile dimension which exists in sight. As for the child, it explores the world, but it does not go round in circles within a dwelling, the outside of which amounts to the inside. It goes and reconnoitres, and its thirst for knowing is almost infinite.

No doubt, it is regrettable that the environment in which the child carries on investigating is more and more made up of fabricated objects and not of living beings. Indeed, beyond the fact that its perception is then partial, its vitality also fails for lack of energetic communication or communion with what it approaches. And if sight and touch remain the senses most solicited, it would be relevant to wonder about what sorts of looking and touching are then in question. Are they perceptions in which a reciprocity remains effective or, instead, a first attempt to master and take possession of the world by a budding technocrat? If the child opens out to a world which is no longer opening to it, what will happen to its own becoming? Will it turn into a demiurge lacking energy (cf. 'On the Essence and Concept of phases in Aristotle's *Physics B, I*' in *Pathmarks*) Only living beings come into presence by themselves and offer the little child, who opens up to them, their own opening to its world. The meeting between the young explorer and pieces of its environment ought to correspond to, or at least render possible, an articulation between two worlds, the fitting of which is provided by life itself. In this way neither the world nor the little human will dominate over one another in a kind of conflicting dilemma between subjectivity and objectivity. Different appearances of life will fertilize one another, and the opening up of the child to the world will contribute towards its own blossoming as living—which cannot occur if the child is surrounded only by fabricated objects, the existence of which already amounts to human work and does not provide a living presence and energy in a will. The relationship of dominating–dominated then risks being the one which organizes the world in which the child is situated; and, if it enjoys a power, at least a virtual power, over its surroundings, because this results from a human making, it is also a slave to this world as, for a greater part, it meets its needs and thus it cannot do without it. Moreover, instead of opening up to it, as a living world can do, such a fabricated universe commands not only the child's needs, but also its gestures and even its thoughts (cf. Jean Paul Sartre, *Being and Nothingness*, Third Part, Chapter III, Section III).

The impact on structuring of its own being and its own world is thus quite different according to whether the child meets a universe of fabricated objects or a universe of living beings. Only the latter are able to constitute an environment which makes possible the development of its living properties, especially at the level of sensibility and communication, notably providing it with energy it needs for this.

Resources for such a growing are, or ought to be, particularly substantial for meeting other humans. Alas! these others are also endowed with a greater capacity for surviving by cutting themselves off from their natural belonging, which deprives them of their vital potential and even renders them unable to offer the child a model of blossoming faithful to its nature.

Another thing determines the manner according to which the child begins inhabiting the world. The movements of other living beings are first and foremost inspired by their needs: food need, shelter need and, later, the need to reproduce. Now the child does not move with such purpose because its family circle or other members of its surroundings provide for its basic needs. Thus, why does it move? Because it is necessary for it to move? Because it wants to know? Whereas other living beings move, horizontally or vertically, in order to answer merely physical requirements, the movements of the child obey requirements which are in a way meta-physical. And its longings are almost infinite.

Once again, they are the suppliers of what it needs who will set limits to its impulses: spatial and temporal limits to what it is allowed or forbidden to explore.

And if the little child sometimes weeps because it is really hungry, quite often it also cries when it is taken away from its explorations because it is time for eating—and this reaction is particularly frequent when it is removed from the natural world. All the soothing words which are then pronounced do not succeed in calming its sorrow or its anger at being removed from its aspirations and reduced to mere needs. Taking it back home, into a human shelter, is not an easy task either. If the little child is happy with finding itself in familiar surroundings, it does not easily agree with its world being limited to what is already known and common: it wants to go beyond the world already familiar and ruled by its milieu. It longs for more, save when it remains in a natural environment.

Unfortunately, it is dependent on adults who do not, or too little do, imagine what a little child wants. Of course its insatiable longing may put it in danger. If a living being moves in itself, by itself and towards itself—as Heidegger comments in his text 'On the Essence and Concept of phúsis in Aristotle's Physics B, 1'—the child does not clearly realize what 'towards itself' means. And its limitless desire for moving to explore may lead it astray from a possible return to itself, within itself and so jeopardize its own development.

It is also true that people who care for the baby do not worry very much about how to help the child to perceive its limits, instead of imposing on it limits which are not exactly its own, and without explaining to it that what is required of it corresponds to its necessities. Furthermore, these once more are viewed almost exclusively in terms of needs and not as spiritual longings already existing in the baby. For example, who takes into consideration its breathing at a level which has nothing to do with a mere survival, and communicates with it on this subject? Who notices, and tells it, with encouraging and creative words, about its different approach to the world according to whether it is a boy or a girl? However, we have just to observe their behaviours to note that the way of meeting beings is not the same for boys and girls, and that their manner of living space and time is different too. This is not surprising given that sexuation, beginning with the body's morphology and what it presupposes as relational identity, determines a specific threshold and framework, starting from which the child enters into the world and perceives it. Paying attention to and cultivating these properties would be a way of not subjecting the child to physical needs alone and of awakening a potential that exceeds the limits of needs but is not, for all that, undifferentiated and without limits, including material limits.

5

Dwelling in Oneself

How could we inhabit the world without dwelling in ourselves? This question underlies many philosophical developments and cultural discourses in the broad sense of the term, but it is not yet solved for all that. Indeed, our tradition stresses our relation with the outside more than the inside of us and their articulation with one another. It even renders our conception of human being and of its consciousness as dependent on the perception and elaboration of a real external to us to the detriment of our inner self—in an exemplary way in Hegelian dialectics, and which was already established in early Greek culture. Human being in a way became lost in the world, whatever its claim to master it, without a possible return to itself, without building a passage between the outside and the inside of its self. Hence the projection of this self onto the world and the incorporation of the world into the self, two processes which prevent us from inhabiting or dwelling both in the outside and in the inside. In other words, they prevent us from being able to stay in ourselves through recognizing the otherness of the other and the fecundity of meeting with all sorts of others that constitute the world.

Merleau-Ponty writes that 'the body as a model of sensibility makes possible to the one who inhabits and feels it to feel all that which is

© The Author(s) 2017

L. Irigaray, *To Be Born*, DOI 10.1007/978-3-319-39222-6_5

similar to it in the outside' so that 'the body unites us directly to things through its ontogenesis by binding together the two parts of which it is made, its two lips, the sensitive mass that it is and the sensitive mass in which it was born by segregation, to which it remains open as seeing' (cf. 'Interlacing and chiasmus', in *The Visible and the Invisible*, p. 136; I use my own translation in all the quotes to this chapter of *The Visible and the Invisible*). He continues asserting that as 'the one who sees is situated in what is seen, it is still oneself that one sees (and that) there is a fundamental narcissism in every sight' (idem, p. 139). However, such narcissism paradoxically ends up in 'an innate anonymity of myself' that Merleau-Ponty sometimes calls 'flesh', a flesh which participates in the universality of the flesh of the world (idem, p. 137). This is so much so that, given the complicity, not to say assimilation, between seeing and touching in his discourse, Merleau-Ponty can write 'why touching the hand of an other, would I not touch the same power to espouse forms as when I touch my own hand' because 'they both belong to the same space of consciousness and one man only touches a single thing through the two' and 'the other bodies being known by me as my own, it is also with the same world that they and I ought to deal' (idem, p. 141).

Such badly differentiated and in a way mechanical experience of the world by a 'Sentient in general before a sensible in general' (idem, p. 142) neglects the specificity of what happens in the perception of a human or not human living being, instead of the mediation of the sensory percep-tions. If it is 'underpinned by the pre-reflexive and pre-objective unity of my body' (idem, pp. 141–42), it does not for all that have a part in the motion of life itself in which every moment and every space are experi-enced by one body being irreducible to any other and which requires each to respect the interval—of air, of breath—of a nothing in common in order to be approached and met, including by the eyes and the hand.

The structure of interlacing and chiasmus that Merleau-Ponty pro-poses as a model of relating to the world amounts to a universe in which the sentient properties of living end in being subjected to a logic which neutralizes them by removing them from the singularity of their source. Fortunately, our small child does not explore the world in this way. But what listening-to and cultivation of its experience will allow it to remember its original approach to the world and to constitute an inner world, respectful of the limit between the outside and the inside. Such a world could participate in the elaboration of a subjectivity in which what is already familiar does not prevent an opening of oneself to the beyond of the already lived and does not lead to a possible substitution between those who are presumed to be sharing the same experience, especially the tactile one.

To inhabit the world cannot mean immersing oneself in a world impersonal and lacking in differentiation in which each melts and merges into what it approaches and touches, and also with those who approach and touch the same forms of the same world. Such an experience will result in being haunted by a world in which, moreover, one wastes away because of ennui, disgust, melancholy and weariness, states which are well known and extensively commented on by philosophers, novelists or everyday people over recent centuries. And if we want to provide a future for humanity, we must urgently suggest another manner of living the relation to ourselves and to the world, and the relation between ourselves and the world.

Heidegger's thought can supply us with elements to rethink our relation to and with the world, especially when he invites us to reappropriate the world so that we experience it in a more genuine manner and when he tells us to return to a *phusis* from which our tradition has wandered so far that we forget what it means to be living. Heidegger speaks about coming into the world of a human being as that of 'a being deprived of itself and handed over by the world' (cf. *Being and Time*, Third Chapter, Section 17, and also Walter Biemel, *Le concept de monde chez Heidegger*, especially the Second Part), a world that we must little by little reappropriate in order to make it suitable for ourselves. Being abandoned to the world means living one's own being in accordance with beings which surround us and which constitute the world of everyone so that we become a someone amongst others who, furthermore, do not even belong to our time. The world into which we are thrown or abandoned is an impersonal one, in which we get lost in a being-with which does not consider the authentic or real being of the elements which constitute it, in particular our own.

If Merleau-Ponty seems to affirm that the world in which we are situated is our present creation, such a conception of the world does not equate to that of Heidegger. Nor does the latter think, as Merleau-Ponty suggests, that the world turns over to us so that we are in a way enclosed in our own reflection or image, even if some of his words about language, and also about Being, have something to do with such a discourse. For Heidegger, the world to which we are handed over has been constituted as it is now by a previous history in which being and Being, including ours, gradually turned away from us and became forgotten by us so that we find ourselves in a world which is extraneous to us and that we must little by little reappropriate.

The matter is thus not one of forcing the child to adapt itself to the world but, instead, of allowing it to transform this world according to its potential and its desire. Its presence must make a breach in the world as it already is; it has not to conform to it but to reopen its totality and its horizon—to spatialize it anew, one could say—to disclose it or let it take form(s) according to its own dynamism. This requires that the natural dynamism of the living being is recognized and cultivated—in its growing, its way of unfolding and blooming. If the words of Merleau-Ponty appear to prompt a sort of placental regression, those of Heidegger instead invite us to repeat the motion of opening that being born means. Of course the matter is no longer one of clearing a passage for leaving the maternal body or for opening one's own body in order to procure for oneself the air one needs through breathing. Rather the matter is one of reopening the horizon which results from our culture, and in which we are imprisoned, towards a new relation to earth and sky, to mortals and gods, to quote Heidegger. This permits us to discover and create living bonds with our surroundings with a being-with in mind which is not limited to a mere juxtaposition or interweaving of beings into a constructed totality. In reality, we have to open a clearing in a space filled with beings and their interrelations so that light can come into it again and enlighten us on the world to which we are handed over in order that we can interpret and transform it to make it more authentically ours.

Once more the question which must be asked is how we can both distinguish and articulate what comes from a natural origin with its properties on the one hand and what comes from a culture suitable for human beings on the other hand. In my opinion, humans must not give up their natural properties, especially their sexuate belonging, in order to authentically inhabit the world. Thinking of their relation(s) to the world as relation(s) in the neuter amounts to an exile from themselves and prevents them from maintaining an authentic relation to the real. Indeed, the apprehension of the world is not neuter but sexuate. For lack of acknowledging this, the child is situated in a fictitious transcendence in relation to the real—Heidegger would say: in an ecstasis regarding the real—a transcendence artificially constructed which cuts it off from an appropriate perception of itself and of the world. To consider a human being to be dependent on a *Dasein* in the neuter, that is asexuate, amounts to abandoning it to a world in which Being—and, consequently, our being in such a conception of the world—can only wander, death defining the limit of its horizon.

It is still with its body that the child goes in search of the world. This body is the frame from which it perceives, moves towards, apprehends. It is the mediator between itself and the world, and the first which provides it with a view of the world. If this did not yet exist, the child could not find its bearings, it would remain prostrated without possibility of turning towards or returning to any place, of choosing some or other direction. There is its body which gives meaning to this first spatialization, and this body is not reduced to its eyes and its hands.

The other senses have a part in the global frame that its body is, as is the case for its sexuation. The little girl and the little boy do not experience space in the same way. The former, more than the latter, attempts to establish a link between the external world and her inner spaces; she already knows that if the world exists outside herself, it also takes place in herself; she also moves more discreetly; she seizes things less, aims at subjecting them to herself less in order to construct or deconstruct the world. The little boy, more than the girl, projects himself towards and onto the world; he tries to find himself in this way: through his explorations, his interventions, his fabrications. He runs more, and his gestures are more brusque and inspired by the desire to appropriate; he externalizes more than the girl. The little boy is more daring and more dependent. It also seems that he makes a more important use of his legs than the little girl, who uses her arms more—to touch gently, to take care of dolls or living beings.

Are all these only stereotypes? If so, then one might as well say that our body amounts to a stereotype, instead of incarnating the different potentials of our genes and chromosomes. The bodily morphology of the child expresses itself in its relations to and with the world, and to forbid it in this way of expressing amounts to depriving it of developing in accordance with the one who it is. This prevents it from giving meaning to the world as well as to its relation(s) to and with the world, and from structuring the latter into an evolving whole without forcing upon it models which paralyse the dynamism resulting from life itself. This renders it also impossible for children to inhabit themselves and to experience the satisfaction of resting in themselves after their explorations of the world, in which sensory perceptions and sexuate belonging are the main language.

Hence there is an infinite wandering of the child outside itself and its need to cling on to some transitional object—a thumb, a teddy bear, a piece of rag—as an accompaniment to reassure itself during its various going through the world (on this subject cf. Winnicott, especially 'Transitional Objects and transitional Phenomena', in *International Journal of Psychoanalysis*, 34: 89–97). The hand of the persons who accompany it, one of their clothes or things, their voices or some of their words, can also act as transitional objects. This reduces the possibility of intersubjective relationships that are capable of marking out space by appropriating a part of the other to help on the solitary journey, in which no real presence provides the child with an opportunity to transcend itself.

Now is this not the meaning of its explorations? Does it not try to exceed itself towards the world, to transcend itself by opening up to what surrounds it, including to the other? And is it not the structure of its body, especially its sexuation, which supplies to it a frame which allows an access to a transcendental perception of the world and of the other that is capable of corresponding to its desire and of giving sense to its movements? Lacking this, will the sense not be other than a mere restlessness, a need to move without making any contribution to the development of the child, which, at this stage, represents for it the means of transcending itself?

6

Being-With

The child moves to open up to the world. If this world is made up of fabricated objects, the child does not meet beings which open up to it and with which it can really coexist. It must seize them one way or another to create a link with them. Thus it will transform them into tools to satisfy its relational need or desire and integrate them into a whole. It also learns to name them in order to organize them into a totality. In the beginning, the relations that the child has with the elements of the world still remain living. It is not yet enslaved, subjected to imperatives which impose on it a certain use of what surrounds it. It discovers the world and it plays with its discoveries to ensure gradually its mastery over them.

Things are different when the child approaches living beings—it cannot seize these so easily. If its perplexity is less aroused by the vegetal world, nevertheless it pauses to consider it. Above all it feels at home and happy in the vegetal world. Generally, it is the environment that the little child prefers, and removing it from these surroundings does not happen easily and brings about cries and anger. It is the place in which it agrees to leave its transitional objects to inquire about life and to try to share it. There, it even gives up its toys. Being in nature is enough for it

© The Author(s) 2017
L. Irigaray, *To Be Born*, DOI 10.1007/978-3-319-39222-6_6

as well as playing with what nature offers to it—being filled with it through breathing, through its skin and all its senses. It delights in communing totally with it by touching grass, smelling a flower, sheltering under a tree or climbing it, marveling at a ray of sunshine. It stands in this whole that the garden, or some other natural place, is without intending to structure it into a whole. It finds in nature a sort of home where it enjoys being and would like to stay. Unfortunately, its human vulnerability prevents such wanting from being fulfilled and brings it once more back to its needs: for a shelter during the night, against bad weather or eventual attacks from other living beings, especially from certain animals.

Thus the child must leave the garden, the woods or whatever natural sojourn to take shelter in a place built by man, where life is protected and maintained, but not really cultivated as such. And it is the same for bodily properties which call for a being in relations with the other; for example, breathing, sensory perceptions and sexuation, which are poorly considered in this regard. Being together is then determined by concern about satisfying natural needs and a coexistence ruled by sharing the world as it is, beginning with that of the family home. Partaking in life within such a place is quite different from what happens in nature; in reality, life itself is not really shared in the family house. Family community is first based on survival and its material requirements as well as on the forms with which they are endowed. Its finality is also to favour the reproduction of the human species.

Now it is through family coexistence or its substitutes that the child will experience what being-with means. Obviously this being-with is not without qualities, but these do not correspond to what life involves at its most natural and transcendental levels. In reality, the behaviours that Heidegger analyses, as those of a human being abandoned in a world that it has not yet made its own, amount to those required for coexisting within the family. Being-with is then determined by the conditions for living together in a certain pre-given world, by having in common a same universe, rather than by reaching an authentic being in relation. To relate to things, what is more to others is not favoured by the family background, and the other as other does not really exist in the family community. Indeed this is set up from participants in the same unit, being their being-with then defined by this belonging, including with regard to feelings, rights and the obligations which follow from it. In a way, even the life of each member is no longer peculiar to it but is a property of the family unit, in which none can decide on for personal use, especially for being with an other.

For this to happen, it will be necessary to come out of the enclosure of the family and gain solitude as a living being. This stage is not reached by all humans, and many of them remain dependent on family communities under various guises, be these cultural, religious or political. They take part in a community in which being with is established by participating in the same roots, the same background, the same ideal. They share something which binds them together but without the autonomy and freedom that a real being-with demands of us. If the being-with that procures family can satisfy needs, it does not offer either hospitality or conditions for a culture of our being-with as humans. Instead it divides us between a so-called 'natural part', for which coexistence would not need further differentiation, and a part which is presumed to meet our trans-cendental aspirations and of which the school, the state and the church ensure development, in particular with regard to the child. However, the transcendental potential of natural belonging will then be scarcely con-sidered, assuming that it is not repressed.

No doubt, a culture of relationships exists within the family itself, but it aims less to support the blossoming of the potential of each of its members than to ensure the unity that they form. And the effective aptitudes that Heidegger defines as those of any human with respect to the world into which it comes, can be applied to the family universe of which the world represents a more complex extension. One member of the family exists anyway as belonging to the family and coexisting with those who make it up. It does not exist by itself and, as such, it is its duty to recognize others as constituting the same whole and to adopt towards them an attitude of respect, of concern and of care. These behaviours maintain the functioning of the family unit, the role of which is not to promote heroism and transcendental aspirations of one or the other, but to maintain the coherence of the whole. It is not within the original family or its substitutes that the heroism of the one who gave birth to oneself can be cultivated. A family tolerates transcendence as long as it corresponds with an ideal at once recognized and shared, but not as the exceptional destiny of one of its members. The roots that a family offers are first those belonging to a genealogy, a tradition, an institution from which each will have to become emancipated in order to project itself into a future which is based on a personal desire.

The being-with which takes place inside the family community does not allow for a blossoming of the whole being. In the genesis of a human being, the family cares above all about somatic subsistence and growth, without looking for the total blossoming of the genetic potential. This is presupposed to be preserved by the family, but it is not the place of its complete embodiment. Moreover, in spite of a physical development, its corresponding expression and actualization are not allowed to take place in this circle. The family enclosure does not permit the child to appear totally as it is. It cannot find there both recognition and cultivation suitable for its bodily maturity, especially at a sexual, but even a sexuate, level.

The family favours the genealogical dimension, and it even subjects the development of the individual to this paradigm and to values which are dependent on it: reproduction, authority, verticality, and so on. Only the most material and physical aspect of sexuate identity is considered, the one that can be least actively modified by human cultivation. It is also the one which will contribute to privileging vertical transcendence over horizontal transcendence, and a transcendence which results from genealogical antecedents endowed with power rather than from the spiritual qualities which are required by the recognition of the otherness of the other. In reality, the being-with that is reliant on genealogy is determined by the immaturity of the little child and is not, or ought not to be, characteristic of humanity—and animals are often better than we are in this respect. Had not humanity, to distinguish itself from the animal kingdom, to equip parental authority and genealogical values with a spiritual transcendence which is extrapolated from a divinity extraneous to our earthly life? Conceived in this way does this transcendence contribute towards our being-with or does it harm it? What sort of being-with does it favour, and what other does it thwart?

The cohesion of the family community is ensured by both communing in a barely differentiated natural belonging and sharing the same values, without a passage between these two uniting factors being really guaranteed. Each family member is at once protected and alienated by the unit in which it is integrated. The mood or disposition which is required from each to fit this microcosm does not really send it back to its own existence. The family unit does not allow each to perceive what or who it is and must become; and it is the same with cultural or religious communities which are based on suprasensitive values. Humans are sheltered but also dispossessed of their being by a world which does not situate them in front of themselves and their potential. Humans then turn away from the tragically solitary task that incarnating their own being represents by surrounding themselves with a familiar universe, in which safety is ensured on condition of referring to a beyond of terrestrial life which keeps in abeyance their relation to transcendence. If they gain in comfort and relief from anguish or fear, humans in this way lose some intimacy with themselves and a perception of what might help them to be.

The figure of Antigone embodies aspects of a culture of nature—at the cosmic, generational and sexuate levels—which, as such, contribute towards the preservation and development of human being. As belonging to a family community, humans must then adopt an ethical behaviour fitting in the respect for nature and its cultivation, instead of subjecting it to abstractly moral rules extraneous to the natural order. Contrary to the lack of individuation and the neutralization of each member resulting from the passage to the patriarchal family order, the ethical laws of the matrilineal tradition guarantee respect for the place essential to the life of every human and non-human living being, and also stress the particularity of each individual, safeguarded especially by its sexuation and its corresponding role in generation. When the family world becomes a unit which is not really based on natural laws and in harmony with the cosmic universe it no longer offers to each either an understandable range of its potentialities or the means of elaborating plans which allow it to realize them. The safety at the level of needs that the family institution provides is offset by a lack of power to be for each member as well as by the reduction of communication and communion between all the members in a unit in which what is useful prevails over the blossoming of the relationships, especially the sensitive and affectionate ones. Which prevents a real being-with from happening.

7

To Become Oneself

Becoming oneself is a complex undertaking for a human. For a plant, it occurs naturally if the environment is adequate. The seed of a tree supplies roots and the programme of its becoming without external intervention being necessary. The 'face' of the tree corresponds to a growth determined by the seed itself, as Aristotle writes (cf. *Physics*, B, 1, 12–13). For a human being, things are really more complex because its taking root is not so simple. Undoubtedly its genetic programme is given to it, originally; but not the way of incarnating it. A human being is a determined living being whose blossoming is dependent on its determination. But how to cultivate the living being that each human is? The first and perhaps most radical failing of our culture is that it intends to start from human being as such. Now this being does not correspond to a living being but to an idea or a constructed entity. A human, as living, is differentiated, especially by its sexuation. And if, as Aristotle teaches us, '*phusis* develops towards *phusis* by means of *phusis*', then omitting to recognize human being as being a man or a woman amounts to removing it from the natural dynamism which allows it to accomplish itself. In Aristotelian terms, one could say: this prevents it from entering into presence with a face flowered from a dynamism—a *dunamis*—of its own.

© The Author(s) 2017
L. Irigaray, *To Be Born*, DOI 10.1007/978-3-319-39222-6_7

Human beings resort, for their development, to a fabricated paradigm which has no energy by itself. Imposing it on a boy or a girl, as a way or a model towards their becoming means destroying the dynamism conforming to their living being. Consequently, they lose the source of their natural energy and the possibility of growing in accordance with it. It is thus understandable that humans consider earthly sojourn as an exile and not a place where they can blossom. They have become a kind of fabricated product, the functioning of which is ruled by suprasensitive patterns and ideals extraneous to their real being and which are impracticable by them. Without either an origin or an end that is faithful to their original being, they indefinitely wander, hoping they will experience fullness in the beyond. One could say that they do not really exist, if existing signifies fulfilling one's own being.

Moreover, as it is cut off from the origin of the evolution of its becoming, human being is paralyzed in its development. Indeed, this asks of each a constant return to its source in order to achieve better and better their own. Without a continual movement of backwards and forwards between one's beginning and one's end, no one can accomplish one's own becoming; and this quest, which is based on a natural dynamism, risks becoming a going around in circles—a sort of eternal return of the same—in which energy exhausts itself, and which ends in a nothing (of) being. If, for a human, returning to the origin of being is a search without end, then it must also be wary about not reversing this search into a limitless projection of itself, into an infinite opening in which its own being exhausts itself. It must discover how to become faithful to the one who it is in a way which contributes, even indirectly, to the achievement of this being. Of course, the matter is not one of reducing our being to what we do or make—as Jean-Paul Sartre would like—because we might so wander more and more from whom we are and become a kind of dangerous nomad, as much for others as for ourselves. We also risk mistaking the gesture of transcending, and transcending ourselves, for a projection into the distance or into the beyond. And this prevents us from actively caring about our development by continuously transcending ourselves.

How can we carry out such an undertaking without cutting ourselves off from ourselves, given that we are uprooted from our birth, if not from our conception? We have been conceived by two but we are only one, even if we embody something of the two who have conceived us through our genes and chromosomes. The first place in which we develop and move, from which we receive oxygen, warmth and food, is our mother from whom we part by being born. From our birth, we begin moving by ourselves: at the level of growing and, soon, at the level of movements in space, and —we then become, at least partly, all what we meet. Furthermore, models extraneous to our natural belonging are imposed on us.

How can we become ourselves in spite of such uprooting? It seems that we have to procure roots for ourselves without mistaking the circumstances of our birth and our first childhood for our roots. This, once more, would amount to sacrificing to mainly occasional situations our transcendental potential, letting it be encysted into a familiarity determined by needs, habits, customs and a dependence upon things or others. Given the anguish that uncertainty and the gap with regard to our origin arouse in us, we frequently confuse what relates to our origin and to our real potential.

Our literature, and even our philosophy and religion, are often inspired by a feeling nostalgic for what is connected with childhood, whether nostalgia expresses itself as an insuperable melancholy or whether it takes the form of a romantic overestimation of the places and sensations linked to our childhood or of an unconditional celebration, including a religious celebration, of the newborn, if not of the foetus—as the enchantment that Christmas awakens in the world shows. The fact that the transcendental potential of the little child has not been taken into consideration and could not be embodied, given its physical immaturity, probably results in its projection onto the places, and even the times, of its potential manifestation, without a possible embodiment, by the one who was its source. It can also be sensed as a treasure or a mystery which would have been concealed in these places and times and of which we would be in search of as what would allow us to achieve our destiny. As the object or issue of our quest is indefinitely hidden from our apprehension, we invest in the place which is presumed to hold it, instead of detecting something of its enigma buried in ourselves and trying to unveil it by existing, without yet being able to appropriate it completely.

Human being cannot incarnate what corresponds to its genetic inheritance with a single motion, as a tree can do. The complexity of its origin and of its movements in space as well as its additional neurons thwart the simplicity and continuity of plant growing. If it is suitable that human being remembers such a natural growing, it, for itself, must assist its development with other productions than the growing by itself of the tree. The 'itself' of a human being is hidden in the indiscernible nature of its origin, and its manner of existing continuously separates it from this origin. Only indirectly can it perceive something of the latter and, so, attempt to return to itself. The question is how to avoid reflecting during this return in order to come back to a natural source of energy.

To invest one's energy in a work is a possible way of being faithful to oneself and discovering one aspect of one's own face. This presupposes that one creates without an external model, as an endeavour to embody the one who one is through shaping a work. Such an undertaking is not simple, and a child is at once more and less capable of carrying it out than an adult. Anyway it is advisable to encourage it to go this way without reserving this sort of practice only as a therapy for those who are presumed to be mentally ill. Incentive can be supported by resorting to that on which the desire of the child focuses so that a production of vital or affective energy can combine with transcendental aspirations. In this way, the body unites with soul or spirit, as well as the present with the past and the future. Projecting itself into a work, human being becomes revealed through a making—a *poiesis*—which allows it, if not to return to itself, at least to invest its energy in a manner that does not separate it too much from itself, as happens through the subjection to or consumption of products made by others than itself.

Some mythological figures, such as Narcissus, but also some theoreticians such as the psychologist Henri Wallon or the psychoanalyst Jacques Lacan, have thought that appropriating one's self can occur by seeing one's mirror image. No doubt this is a means for the child to perceive itself apart from its surroundings, in particular from its mother. However, does specular identification not contribute to cutting it off from its living roots? Does the mirror image not isolate the child from a living environment, from others, and even from itself? Does it not bring about a sort of ecstasis with respect to the natural development which, furthermore, acts as a sort of confinement given the inversion of the self that the process of reflection involves? If the mirror image seems to favour individuation, does this not exist to the detriment of a growth which is achieved thanks to relations to and with other, human or non-human, living beings? Is it not through the cultivation of such relations that individuation can be won, notably by learning how to respect difference(s)? In other words, it is not its mirror image, or its projection onto some idols, which can lead the child to the discovery of itself, and perhaps no more a reflection starting from representations, notably because these approaches take up energy without providing it in return. What could be the short-lived satisfaction that they can procure for a living being, they are not of use for its development and that of the environment in which it lives.

Our way of behaving attempts to grasp and fix the mystery of our origin into a face, whereas we ought always to abandon any face that has already appeared so that we can develop. We can remain living only at the price of a continuous becoming, which means relinquishing what is already flowered, which falls into appearance as soon as it has appeared. Faithfulness to itself of a human being cannot content itself with one presence, one reproduction or representation. Life cannot settle in one form only, it ceaselessly grows in different forms on pain of being already, at least in part, death.

In fact the 'know thyself' of Socrates amounts to an injunction to begin dying while living. Knowing oneself can occur only through one's work and the return to oneself as the place where life is preserved and from which it can still germinate. This needs a being with oneself free from representation or knowledge already determined—a repose in oneself of breath, of energy, without any intention or plan; that is, an attempt to go back to the source of our living being, in order to perceive it and let it be and spring up, instead of drying up through our existence.

This stage is essential in order not to become confused with every-thing or everyone we meet; not to become objects, customs, ideas, individuals that surround us; not to fall, or fall again, into the lack of differentiation of a 'one'. Becoming oneself means winning this unique being that we are, but of which our culture and the milieu in which we live constantly deprive us. It means discovering the sole and irreducible nature of our own being and caring about cultivating it as such towards its blossoming, however difficult the task may be. Indeed, becoming oneself requires one to give up the quietness that the fact of assimilating to the world in which we stay brings to ourselves and to take on the anguish of solitude and decisions on the way to follow in order to favour a development which is both suitable for us and concerned with what and who partake in our existence. And this asks of us to distinguish ourselves from them so that we become capable of respect for their own being.

Becoming oneself requires as much heroism as being born, and also needs resorting to our breath in order to emerge from the family and sociocultural background which, too often, substitute themselves for the maternal placenta in which we started living. It is a matter of winning an existence of our own again.

8

Language to Produce Something or to Produce Someone?

It is commonly accepted that the human is the living being capable of speech; or that 'speech enables man to be the living being he is as man'; or even that 'it is as one who speak that man is man' (cf. Heidegger quoting Humbold in the text 'The Word' in Poetry, Language, Thought, p. 185). These kinds of affirmations seem to go without saying, at least in the West, and they remind us of the human destiny that we are in charge of carrying out. What then about Buddha who attempted to reach silence as the path towards the accomplishment of humanity? Could the Buddha's quest be the mere complement, or even the reverse, of what a Westerner considers to be the achievement of the human lot? Or is something else at stake? Would not Buddha try to carry out his natural growth whereas, in the Western tradition, human development could be achieved only by interrupting the continuity with our natural belonging and entering into the universe of discourse? In the West, gathering oneself together could occur only after a leap with respect to our origin, which makes us born from the word itself, whereas, in other cultures, such gathering remains more similar to that of a bud or, better, to the capacity of certain flowers for alternating the opening

© The Author(s) 2017
L. Irigaray, *To Be Born*, DOI 10.1007/978-3-319-39222-6_8

out and the closing up of their corollas, blooming and going back to withdraw into an invisible sap.

Are humans capable of such gestures to accompany their becoming or do they need speech for this purpose? An what speech? It seems that speech for us has been elaborated as a universe parallel to life, that it claims to say the living without the living expressing itself through it. Certainly the cry of the newborn, which goes with the first breathing, is a word which says it; and the same goes for its babbling. It is really the baby that is spoken and speaks to us through it, as is the case concerning the humming and tears of the little child, and the stories that sometimes it tells to us or even its questions. The loving, faltering stammering or moans are also words sent out by living beings as well as the groans of the ill, or some mystical orisons or hymns addressed to God by fervent believers. The shouts of laughter also talk to us sometimes. But does the language that has been taught us and that we are supposed to use as living humans express us? Or is this language above all of help as a tool to appropriate all that which surrounds us and bend it to our use? Is the function of speech to appropriate the world or to contribute to a becoming that is appropriate to us? Does our culture care about this second purpose enough, even though it ought to correspond with its first purpose, and so distinguish human being from other living beings? Ought not the meaning of speech to accompany and support the motion of growing that is specific to humanity? Is not its significance to enable the life of humans to flower? Yet, does it not act more often than not as what cuts us off from life instead of making it blossom as human? What could be the speech that tells human being?

Has not our culture once more torn us between a word of divine origin and a word that is of use for satisfying our needs (cf. on this subject the Prologue of the Gospel According to St John), neither of which telling human being as such? Ought not this telling to be a bridge between the universe of needs and that of desires, the former being more purely material and the latter more spiritual, the former ultimately likely to do without speech and the latter requiring us to resort to word? But are we not yet lacking this word? Would the division into body and soul have meaning if this were not the case? And would then spirit be limited to learning words already said, that is, to a subjection of our existence to the past? Is it not up to us to live in the present thanks to our own words?

If we cannot flower as a vegetal being does, has not the word to contribute to the possibility of our becoming present in the present? Must it not grant us a presence here and now, whatever our lack of roots? Is not the word that which ought, at least in part, to compensate for this lack instead of increasing our being exiled from our origin? Indeed the word is not merely spoken by humans, it also speaks by itself and, as such, generates itself and ends in creating a world of its own which does not correspond to that of our natural development—of our *phuein*. The word which could accompany and favour the latter is still lacking. For example, we have not yet thought about the properties of our speaking which would make it capable of acting as the elements necessary for our physical growth: air, sun, water, earth. Now this function of speech is possible (*Through Vegetal Being* 'my part of the Chapter' Could gestures and words substitute for he elements? in Through Vegetal Being, pp. 79–83). We have both overestimated and underestimated the potential of the word. Between its role of tool at our disposal and its identification with the divine or the philosophical logos, it has lost its capacity for being a sort of sap participating in the cultivation of our life here and now, and not only in awakening us to another life, as Jesus's words would come to act according to the Gospels (cf. the Prologue of the Gospel According to St John, and some other passages of the Gospels, e.g. the dialogue between Jesus and the Samaritan, which could be interpreted in this way).

We have neglected the aptitude of speech for feeding our existence and helping us to incarnate ourselves. Speech has been of help to designate the real in order for us to be able to use it. Too often we mistook appellation by a word for appealing for being and being together, an appeal which ought to be directed in a privileged way to another living human, one whose word ought to assist becoming, entering into presence and sharing being. In the use of speech, the stress on the appellation of inanimate beings to ensure their permanence, memory and insertion into a discourse, a logos, aiming at constituting the real into a totality, has caused the forgetting of its role as a call directed to the other. Hence, speech has supported only a stage of our relations to language and of our cultural becoming, this connected with its function as tool and its informative potential, to the detriment of its most human role: ensuring communication between living humans. Word has thus worked towards a split subject–object, instead of being the possibility of relationships between subjects, as well as of a subjectivity resulting from them. It stopped subjectivity at a phase of its development, this corresponding with an attempt to master the real, without reaching the one of being in communication or communion with other, human or non-human, living beings. Too often, being endowed with language not only did not contribute to our natural growth, but also deprived it of the resources of life and energy that it could receive in relating to other living beings.

How to discover another way of speaking, one in which the word does not generate itself without intertwining with our natural development? How to get the word not to define our being-with as co-belonging in the same, discourse or world, but to allow each of us to communicate with the other while letting this other and ourselves be in the world that is suitable for each, without subjecting both to a unity or totality extraneous to our own?

And what words can we speak to the child or suggest that it addresses us, words which invite it to come into the world and share that world with us? Indeed, it is in the relations between two living beings that such production of words can be discovered, which at once contribute to the blossoming of each one, especially thanks to exchanges with the other, but which also allow each one to gather itself together in the deepest intimacy of its being, which corresponds to silence. These words help us to combine—while fitting together, Heidegger perhaps would say—our transcendental aspirations with our physical potentialities, so that human being does not remain everlastingly immature in comparison with what it can and must be.

Only for God would it be possible to be the one who he is. However, granting God such a possibility presupposes that we sense what being oneself means; otherwise, how could we imagine that God is the one who he is? This requires language to be used in order us to appropriate to ourselves more than for appropriating all beings, even on the pretext of rendering them appropriate to themselves—to allude to the considerations of Heidegger about a logical economy of 'appropriation'. Speech must be used for making us appropriate to us as body and soul or spirit, as humanity and divinity, creating the environment in which passing from one dimension to another can and must happen. It must carry out in us the articulation between these parts of us that it separated in the past, that is, bring flesh to spirit, breath to our body, so that we can exist and blossom as humans. In this sense, language cannot correspond to a gathering of more or less arbitrary signs coded in such a way that they are presumed to be capable of representing the real and structuring it into a whole. If the language that we speak can be reduced to such a function this implies that it is a sort of technical implement to which we resort to produce something outside of ourselves, rather than it being of help to produce ourselves as humans. Which would imply it taking root in us and having its finality in us without subjecting us, and moreover subjecting itself, to another end.

In reality, language ought to be a place of resource in words which could assist us in transforming our natural belonging into a human identity, in modelling our energy so that it can perform the passage from our vital to our spiritual destiny. Language ought to help us to succeed in carrying out what a tree can do without resorting to any word: achieving what it is by the transformation of its roots into flowers and fruits. Our lack of continuously taking root in a ground and an atmosphere which are appropriate to us requires us to resort to language in order to compensate for them, to feed us and accompany us, from the most physical to the most spiritual aspects of our existence.

We still lack such language, as we still lack the words which would allow us to go from the most intimate to the most opened out of ourselves, and to adjust the most close to the most remote. Speech has been assimilated to a tool that is useful for us to know the world, to dominate it, to construct it, without us caring enough about its contribution to our own shaping and our becoming. It is so much so that our human being has ended up in being a product of the human or divine word, instead of being a natural living capable of producing word(s) in order to contribute to our achievement, our blossoming.

In reality speech is produced by our body, but we do not use it to develop shapes from our physical belonging, to enable our body to speak.

We reduce it to a machine reproducing a learned code instead of learning how our body could take place as the origin of word(s). As a living being it has energy for that purpose, and speech ought to be a way of expressing and cultivating this energy, notably through passing from its opening up to the world to its gathering with itself, in itself.

Giving the word to our body is a potential of language that we have still to discover. This potential exists and ought to be developed, even before any syntax aiming at joining a subject and an object, as a predication without any object escorting and assisting our becoming—as a way of saying our being (cf. my chapter 'What the vegetal world says to us' in the volume *The Language of Plants*, co-edited by Monica Gagliano, John Ryan and Patricia Vieira). Such saying is not necessarily articulated in words, but it performs and structures our: I live, I exist, I grow, I become, and even I will, I desire, I love. It helps us to build a living bridge between the past, the present and the future, without stopping this process, especially by terms which fix it and prevent it from evolving. It assists us to become what and who we are, to go from the stage of early infancy to that of childhood, of adolescence and adulthood in their various phases.

Before focusing on 'that is' or 'it is', such word tries to say 'I am', preserving in this way the world and ourselves from getting lost in blur, lack of differentiation or assimilation, which remove each of us from our own growth. Before using a dialectical process in order to determine, or restore, the respective truth of subjectivity and objectivity, we need a speech which acts as a dialectics, going from an aspect of ourselves to another and attempting to structure them into a whole, the elements of which do not paralyse one another.

To win some power, role or function does not necessarily contribute towards our living becoming, and a word faithful to life ought to warn us against this, to protect us against such a mistake. Language is a necessary condition for our blossoming as humans, but it cannot accomplish this task if it does not correspond to a living word—a word which says us in the present, in faithfulness to the past and to prepare the future, with the will to achieve our human destiny.

9

The Source of the Word

The various modalities of language can give assistance to our becoming. Unfortunately some of them have disappeared in most tongues. For example, the middle voice no longer exists, which allowed us to go from a more physical self-affection—through a touching of our lips, our eyelids or our hands to one another, helping us to withdraw within ourselves and commune with ourselves—to a saying of this gesture or this state which permitted us to experience self-affection otherwise. The middle voice contributed to a global constitution of the self escaping the alternative between the active and the passive, which entails a relation of the subject to an object or to the other which fundamentally deprives us of an autonomous existence, thus of really relating to and with one another. The middle voice was, and remains, a modality of the word which makes possible both 'to be' and 'to let be', two modes of being of which our human development needs and, thanks to which, time and space can unite with one another from a bodily experience. The middle voice inscribes in our growing a specifically human temporality which allows us to be in harmony, or to part from an immediate communion, with natural rhythms, and even with the other. It builds a sort of place in which we can dwell, which does not amount to a confinement into the 'house

© The Author(s) 2017
L. Irigaray, *To Be Born*, DOI 10.1007/978-3-319-39222-6_9

of language' of Heidegger, but is an opportunity for us to inhabit ourselves—our body, our heart, our soul or spirit, being the elements supplying matter and form(s) to such dwelling that the middle voice tries to express with words. In this way, it removes our affects from a mere instinctive or impulsive economy, and makes our body speak, which then affects itself, is moved, unites with itself, before any separation between subjectivity and objectivity. Uniting with oneself in a sort of scansion, which does not involve definitive inclosing, is also a process which, ensuring a unity for each, renders possible a being in two with regard for their respective difference(s).

It is not by chance that the lexical and grammatical forms expressing 'to be two' in the Greek language disappeared at the same time as the middle voice. For instance, the word *heteros*, the other of two at once the same and different beings—the other lip, the other eye, the other hand, but also the other sex—originally existed, as well as the grammatical forms of the dual which were used for a plural constituted of only two elements. Now these forms are necessary for passing from the solitary self-affection that can happen with the lips, the hands, the eyelids touching one another to the self-affection that can exist between two sexuate bodies in kissing or embracing. This represents a crucial stage in going from oneself as individual to community without losing the possibility of staying in oneself that self-affection grants. If the word lacks for expressing the critical stage of being (in) two—something that Nietzsche perhaps would call 'the relation in two between two loners'—it is unable to say human being in its global nature. It exiles it from itself instead of allowing it to dwell in itself while opening up to the world and to the other. Hence, our being in the world can be only unauthentic, as Heidegger writes, and we cannot recover its authenticity without going back to the time of our culture when the growth of our natural belonging, of our *phuein*, was not yet alienated and lost in a language defined by what is common to a group, a society. Consequently, language becomes a tool useful for representing what exists in such a context and for exchanges about it, in general and independently of personal experience. Then what occurs as self-affection in a relationship between two different living beings is excluded from speaking as well as the connexion—the syntax and the logic—which is suitable for it and takes place before any representation, mirror reflection or speculation. In such self-affection occurring in two, between two, the one and the other give being to one another without returning to a symbiosis lacking difference(s), without stopping either at an image, reproduction or representation, be they personal or collective. The two do not merge into a natural whole—as Dionysus wanted—and they do not remain for all that enclosed within a skin or a self of their own—in accordance with the desire of Apollo. They unite with one another through a difference which leads each to be what or who it is, while being so only thanks to the other.

Such union is word, the word of the in between the two, which attempts to create the place in which they can meet while remaining distinct. This word—still and always inarticulate in terms, and the silent occurrence of which is made possible by gestures—which at once longs for unity but consents to difference, is the original word, of which any other ought to be born and receive its meaning. Such word, which silently tells desire and the necessity for saying, for being to be said, seems to have been forgotten in our tradition, as is the case with the disappearance of some lexical and grammatical forms which built a linguistic framework in which it could be sensed and sheltered. Together with it then also vanished the quest for an environment in which the depth of our intimacy could be revealed as a longing for a union which could happen without the really heroic deed that the preservation of our difference in relation to the desirable necessitates.

However, for each, to be really exists only with the will to make this word arise, which both unites with and disunites from the other, a word which lies at the source of our 'to be' as an origin at once ignored and forgotten of the sense of the 'is' which underlies all our linguistic steps, trials and errors, in search of our truth and our accomplishment.

Such a word is resourcing, but also tearing, because we cannot appropriate it. If we believe that we could be the subject of the totality of the discourse, the latter would not say all meaning or the origin of meaning. It would amounts only to an aspect of them, the whole and the source of which remain unpronounceable in terms and exceeds the gestures and intentions of one alone or of a community made of the same ones. They lie between two as the non-appropriable origin of meaning that they generate through a conjunction of their irreducible difference(s).

In order for such an advent to be possible, each must remain who and what he or she is and discover the word which is suitable for their natural belonging so that this word gets cultivated. Numerous analyses carried out on spontaneous or semi-spontaneous corpuses gathered from mixed populations of children, adolescents or adults belonging to various socio-cultural backgrounds, show that the language produced by boys and girls, men and women, present significant differences, especially with regard to syntactic structures (cf. various chapters in *Je, Tu, Nous*; in *I Love to You* as well as other texts not yet translated into English). The masculine subject favours subject–object relations, the one to many relations, relations amongst the same ones when sentences express relationships between persons, and also vertical genealogical or hierarchical relations. The feminine subject, for her part, favours relations between subjects, between two and differently sexuate subjects, and also horizontal relations. It is easy to answer those who object that all that is a mere question of stereotypes, which have been taught and have nothing to do with a natural identity, that the latter is accompanied by a peculiar morphology which differently determines our entering into relation with the world and with the other(s). To prohibit us from using a language which expresses this difference amounts to claiming that linguistic codes do not have, and must not have, a connection with the real. What does speaking mean if it is so?

Rather, it is necessary today to give meaning to the word again by making it say the real, and this for various reasons. We have to elaborate a world culture, and for that purpose we must start from a human or non-human universal again. The vital resources of living beings are failing for want of a language which tells and cultivates life. We have to consider and respect difference in order to coexist with all living beings, which requires us to overcome a logic which favours sameness. At the human level, it is thus essential that we take into account our natural difference(s) and the manner through which we can express them thanks to a language that induces us to enter into relations and brings meaning to the world as different.

There are other differences which are characteristic of masculine and feminine discourses: the tense and the mood used; the references to an abstract or a concrete environment; resorting to some or other grammatical or logical categories; the use of language as a tool to build or appropriate the world or as a means to meet between subjects and so on. On the logical plane, it is possible to suggest that masculine discourse is more aporetical and feminine discourse more apophantical, which probably corresponds to their respective preference for subject–object relations and subject–subject relations.

The union between a masculine and a feminine subject keeps in abeyance the specification, in particular the linguistic specification, of the object or of the relation between two sexually different subjects, avoiding in this way an insurmountable contradiction. It also lets appear, even as not visible, what is generated of the elusive in their union.

Thus something occurs which both answers and frustrates the relational longing of each one. The risk is that the masculine subject transforms the woman into an object and that the woman fills in, with the child, the indiscernible presence of which takes place between the man and herself in their being in relations. The union between them requires both to be faithful to the syntactical structure—the linguistic *Gestell*— which is appropriate to them, while agreeing to maintain the predication in abeyance as far as the formulation of an object or the particularity of the relationship is concerned. Then the desire for a union only remains, the object or particularity of which are absolute: he no longer has a present or representable object facing him, and she cannot perceive what other subject she has to deal with. Each must accept that emptiness is the place where, perhaps, that towards which their desire longs will appear in the future which must remain undetermined so that appeal subsists and leads them to an original word.

Making a sign or becoming a sign, that each addresses to the other, corresponds to a 'we have to' transform the juxtaposition of our respective 'is' into the conjunction of a 'to be' in which we assemble our different original beings—one and one—in order to reconstruct or, at least, preserve an original 'to be' that cannot be pronounced but in which the unfolding of the word—and of our being—finds a new surge and a necessity to say the real, which no longer confines itself to designating beings of the world in which we are. Now it is a matter of endeavouring to say ourselves. This necessitates a different language which does not divide intellect from sensitiveness but seeks for the origin of the word in the depths of the intimacy of the flesh, in us and between us. Then the word does not arise from itself, as we cannot become without it: it sources from our desire for uniting one another and grants us rebirth from it.

Such word gives meaning to what we have to say to one another. It makes a sign to each without being able to disclose originally its signification other than as an invitation to be. This can be answered only with hesitation and modesty. Indeed, it is a question about the most intimate disclosure of our 'to be' and of its mysterious sharing that is at stake. How, thus, to venture in such revelation without an extreme concern for our corporeal and spiritual belonging and that of the other? The 'is' or 'to be' that our relationship will dare to make exist can either undo meaning up to its most secret provenance or bring it back to its source and entrust us with a responsibility for it in the present and the future. In reality, it is from this relationship that meaning receives a necessity that any community can bring to it, because word has already lost its bond with the flesh from which it takes its origin and that it is supposed to safeguard and cultivate. If it does not spring from this source, word becomes more or less arbitrary coded sign which provokes our being torn between a more physical sound and a more mental meaning, something that, perhaps, makes our speech an appropriate tool for a metaphysical discourse but not a suitable word for saying, and saying to one another, our global being.

No doubt some linguistic expressions, especially the performative verbs—for example, 'to promise', to quote the one which Searle lingers on at length—remain as what permits the relation between an 'I' and a 'you', thus between two subjects to be spoken, though they call for a more mere mental implication rather than the ancient dual. Moreover, the promise can be formulated with respect to a group, such as politicians at the beginning of their mandate. Some other grammatical forms, like the imperative mood, can also, though not necessarily, give utterance to a relationship between two. Nevertheless, the term *heteros*, which was reserved for designating the other of two, no longer exists. The other, for us, is the Greek *allos*, an other amongst many. It is the same for past specific grammatical forms corresponding to the relation between two which now have to be in the plural, as in the case of more than two subjects. With the disappearance of lexical and syntactic structures which both allowed a relationship between two to happen and arose from this relation, we lost the means of achieving a phase of our development. This harms our human accomplishment, but also impoverishes the resources and meaning of language.

10

A Universe of Knowledge and Duties

Language, as it exists, is above all a tool to define, appropriate, use and share our knowledge. As such it is conceived to introduce us to our environment and milieu by denominating and teaching the properties of the various components which make them up. Our language is a sort of code which indicates to us how to make good use of the world in which we are situated. And the verb 'to be', which somehow or other underlies the foundation of the truth that language passes on to us, above all is used for establishing an objective approach to the elements which form the world and the way of organizing them into a whole. In our logic, the verb 'to be' barely contributes to saying or knowing our being, whereas it ought to be the first knowledge—starting from which we can really discover or institute the objective truth of the various components of the world.

At school, in our culture, the child thus learns what is, or would be, the world, but not what or who it, itself, is. For teaching it what the world is, teachers first instruct it in using language. It is taught how to speak, to read, to write, as one handles a tool, a machine, not to say a weapon, which it will interpose between the world and itself. Its linguistic performance will amount to dominating the world by means of

L. Irigaray, *To Be Born*, DOI 10.1007/978-3-319-39222-6_10

language, and not to becoming appropriate to the specificity of the human condition thanks to speech. Moreover, for many people, there is no difference between the terms of the alternative that I have just evoked: speaking 'to appropriate something' or 'to be appropriate to' as human. Unless 'being appropriate to' means conforming to an already constructed world by human beings but which is not for all that appropriate to them.

Then 'to be appropriate to' amounts to an obligation to imitate at the level of behaviour, as well as at the level of word; that is, to become a sort of monkey or parrot, to allude to the stereotypes connected with the animal kingdom, but not really a human being. Indeed, for that purpose, it would be advisable to make the child aware of what language represents and to induce it to use it in a specifically human way; one might as well say in a way which is not only utilitarian but also creative. And yet what is asked of it is to repeat utterances and not to produce itself meaning through enunciation. The child, who gave birth to itself, can create meaning, but the opportunity of doing this is not given to it, and the creative resources of language are not even revealed to it. Its transcendental potential is, once more, subjected to needs by reducing the word(s) to a tool to appropriate the world or appropriate itself to the world, but not as a means to transcend what already exists, inside or outside itself.

What is asked of the child is to imitate what already is and not to go beyond towards what is still to come. Only a few 'great men', according to Hegel, would have the power to achieve such exceeding, what is more at the highest price. Hegel also claims that the passage from one epoch of history to another cannot occur without war and destruction, something that Freud and most other theoreticians of the psyche after him call the necessary murder of the father, often alluding to certain Greek tragedies that present our cultural background.

Longing for transcending itself will be taken into account by an education system imposed on the child only by keeping in abeyance its development through ideals and absolutes out of its reach or by a presupposed objectivity of the world that has already been elaborated. The manner of continuously transcending itself as a living being is not part of the education that it receives. No teacher instructs it on how to continue developing, notably through a cultivation of its breathing.

And, if it shows too much enthusiasm, it will be invited to temper it in order to submit itself to the sociocultural milieu in which it must be integrated—too important aspiration or creativity is not tolerated. Even the divine, when its domain is tackled, is subjected to a rigorously codified approach, which has little to do with breath. What is at stake is to acquire some knowledge about the world built by predecessors and to become able to reproduce it with discourses obeying the same logic. All the sciences of programmed learning follow the same processes of reasoning. It is unrealistic to believe that mathematics, physics or other so-called hard sciences resort to a really different language: it is the same one which is used with merely different formalizations. It is always a matter of learning a supposedly objective truth by way of symbols and a syntax which permit us to apprehend it.

What its subjectivity really is, how to understand what it lives and the way of expressing its desires towards a possible sharing—none of this truly takes place in educational programmes, in which the child is not considered in its whole. The body, the affects, the emotions or feelings are invited to remain outside of the public space of the school, and the latter will take charge only of their civic or moral moulding, of their subjection to a mental control to which the gymnastic lessons will bring a welcome support. Life, flesh, amorous surges, intersubjective relations are barely taken into account by the education system. They secretly develop without a suitable language as a sort of insurrection against compulsory culture.

In reality, our cultural tradition amounts to what Heidegger would call a global modality of being in the world which is not presented as such and by which the transcendental potential of the child is alienated. The plans corresponding to its own aspirations are subjected to a general vision, including regarding itself, which does not let it either perceive or embody them. It lacks a structure for such processes. The frame from which it must envision the real is imposed on it as a certain mode of being in the world, thus as external and even ecstatic with regard to the one it is. In order to realize that it is, or at least has, by itself a frame which allows it to approach the real, it ought to be initiated into the capacity for calling into question the way in which any being of the world is presented to it, instead of being forced to become well integrated into a certain sort of world. Paradoxically it will be deprived of its transcendental potential in the name of practical preoccupations which determine theoretical learning itself. Indeed, there are more concerns about integration into an already constructed world which govern the education system than concerns about providing the child with the means of cultivating its own potentialities. As a transcendental aim it is compelled to submit to what is already common, that is to say, to give up trying to transcend itself towards becoming the one it is, especially by nature.

Hence, 'transcendental' no longer can correspond to an irreducible difference with regard to being, but amounts to an obligation to sub-scribe to values imposed as sorts of norms. And the distinction between the one who the child already is and the one who it must become vanishes; which renders any truth uncertain, provisional, dependent on a constructed order and not on a personal experience of the real. Truth would be dependent on a logic of supposition—if . . . then—and not on an observation or perception—because it is . . . then. Which implies that we do not think about the real by ourselves, and above all not about ourselves.

No method is suggested to the child to learn how to think about itself. Education does not start from the structure that is provided by an incarnate living being; instead it substitutes for it a frame which amounts to an ontological precomprehension of being(s) in which the child is already implicated as an integral part of a vision of a world which is not its own. What is more, no subject that is taught to it tackles what being a child means as a body, as sensitive and sensory perceptions, as needs and desires, memory and plans, and so on. No one tells it that it must constantly come to a compromise between the force of gravity and the force of attraction, between centrifugal force and centripetal force. And, obviously, it is not made clear to it that its sexuate belonging represents a structure that can act in passing from the self to the world, that it determines a universe of its own which must be considered and cultivated for situating itself and finding its own bearings not only in the pre-given world but also in the con-structed world where it is. The child will remain in the unknowable and the non-appropriable as far as it is concerned. And its dependence on milieu, to which its physical immaturity forced it, is perpetuated by a subjection to those presumed to know a truth that it ought to learn but that, in reality, amounts to an exile from itself, a submission to an infinite number of pieces of information which disclose to it neither what or who it is, nor that it is from what or who it is that it must perceive, inhabit and share the world with measure and moderation.

Even if Heidegger claims that 'man is to himself the ultimate aim', our culture does not initiate us into the way that is suitable for such a perspective. It is true that Heidegger wrongly does not take into account the physiological aspect intervening in knowledge. And yet physiology has a part in the projection of human being onto the world, as Nietzsche maintains. It is probably such involvement in the projection that explains that the world is perceived as a whole with certain properties: the structure and specific qualities of the world result, at least for the most part, from the morphology of the one who projects, especially from one's sexuate belonging. Indeed, if the physiological organism can project onto the world a badly differentiated whole, in some way neutered or neutralized, sexuate identity introduces a structural peculiarity and certain qualities into the projected totality. The question is whether the nature of this projection could be more transhistorical and universal than that of a presumed asexuate identity and so could provide a fundamental interpretation of the world and make us capable of taking responsibility for it, instead of submitting to some ontological a priori to which the child ought to render itself available, to which it ought to open up rather than searching for their origin in itself.

Heidegger—as almost all the philosophers of the West—passes from the individual to the world without wondering about projections onto other humans which, also for them, can ensure unity to the subject. Psychoanalysis has revealed the interest of such projections as a therapeutic method, but they can also play a part in the constitution of the unity of each subject in a way that is perhaps easier to decipher if one pays attention to them, rather than when such projections are made onto the world, because the historical factor—Heidegger would say the involvement of being and Being in history—is then more difficult to interpret and deconstruct.

As the subject as such is not considered to be a necessary theme of education, this maintains a part of the unknowable and of duties which prevent the discovery of truth and freedom in an almost insuperable way. How could we value the relevance of truth and freedom without taking into account that of the perception of the subject? Perhaps what could help the latter to recover a more adequate perception is practising a sort of negative ontology in meeting every being, especially every living being. Then the matter is no longer one of learning how to integrate each being into an already existing totality, but of lingering on it, posing wondering about it and deconstructing what it represents for ourselves until we return to its living singularity, the one which exists before any human making and which develops with forms of its own.

From then on, the possibility of a coexistence between different living beings in which each must incarnate an existence faithful to its own to-be, with respect for all living beings and their mutual fecundity, substitutes for learning how to occupy a place in a hierarchy of beings established according to a human conception and plan. Hence, teaching, notably school teaching, no longer amounts to that of linguistic, scientific or moral codes, but to a manner of dwelling and sharing in order to cultivate life in a human way, one's own and that of other human and non-human living beings.

11

Acknowledgement and Recognition

The immaturity or prematurity of the child does not allow it to exercise from the first the potential of its human being. The fact that it is dependent on others for its survival forces it to be also dependent at a transcendental level. It cannot, from the beginning, rebel against the prevailing culture on pain of death. It must comply with the cultural and moral customs of the milieu in which it was born and, no doubt, this dulls, in a more or less deep and lasting way, its possibilities of being what it is, who it is. Its will to be, its enthusiasm and its urge to surpass itself are invited to restrain themselves, even to be forgotten, and its energy to be invested in permitted behaviours, be they physical, affective or more intellectual. It is so much so that, even at the level of perception, the child will be induced to recognize what it perceives—for example what it sees—instead of being initiated into perceiving by itself. This amounts to saying that all it meets has been beforehand transformed into an object materially or mentally fabricated by humans themselves. A filter of precomprehension thus precedes its approach to the real. And this paralyses its energy, especially its sensitive energy, through an a priori perception presumed to be common, through a moulding which is considered necessary but cuts it off from its source of life and puts it

© The Author(s) 2017
L. Irigaray, *To Be Born*, DOI 10.1007/978-3-319-39222-6_11

into an artificial ecstasy through an imposed communion with the world, with the other, and, firstly, with itself. Of course, being in communion with other living beings with consideration for mutual differences requires a certain break in a continuity lived as a natural one; however, this must be desired by the subjects themselves and serve the cultivation of their life, a thing that, alas, is generally not the case with our current educational methods.

Must we, for all that, criticize, condemn and destroy everything we have learned? Not at all, because this would amount to destroying the past, those who built it and the part of ourselves that has been involved in it. On the contrary, we have to acknowledge what has been, and be capable of giving thanks for what we received. Gratitude releases us from resentment and frees our energy to construct bridges towards the future and to become ourselves, bridges in order that a new humanity can occur (cf. 'On the Tarantulas' in *Thus Spoke Zarathustra* by Nietzsche). Gratitude allows us to remember without being blindly subjected to what already has been and so be weighed down by it, so much so that we may we become ill and our body can no longer assume the mediation between the world, the other(s) and ourselves. Gratitude is also what introduces us into another way of thinking, one which does not confine itself to the use of acquired knowledge, but needs a more global approach to the real, starting from an experience that we can and must have of it. And this authorizes us to question the meaning of the discourse that has been taught us and lays down the law on what the real is, without stopping at mere criticism or destruction of every word that already exists. Gratitude gives back each to each and gets rid of links previously established, which made up a whole, towards working out new relations, new words more appropriate to bear witness to the human or non-human real and to enter into relations with it.

In this way, we are brought back to a more original meaning of the word and are induced to check its pertinence, not by starting from our learning existing codes but from our experience of meeting the world which surrounds us, especially its living elements. We are then inclined to produce another word which attempts to say what, in the present, unites us with the world and with the other(s).

Such a word corresponds to a work—a *poiesis*—which permits us to inhabit the world and enter into living communication with its various components. It will be up to us to make this word communicative without, for all that, subjecting it to codes which are presupposed to be universal and timeless, and thus are not suitable for saying life and its perpetual becoming, as well as the manner of entering into communication or communion with other living beings.

The word that we discover in this way requires us to make two gestures: to recognize what we meet, starting from the instruction that we received about it, from terms by which it has been named, and also to recognize it as what it is for us and with regard to the relations that we have with it in the present. This initiates us into the practice of a double discontinuity: that relating to the universe of knowledge and culture in which we are situated and that relating to an immediate experience of the real, especially as living. According to me, this double gesture introduces us into a human cultivation of life which makes possible our own development and our coexistence with other living beings, be they human or non-human.

For this purpose, we have to face a double negative, a double gesture of distanceing, of differing from an immediate experience: that of a familiarity with the world due to our culture and that of a merely sensory or sensitive experience, of an empathy or intensely close meeting with the world in the present. A great part of education henceforth must necessarily consist in giving up any a priori constitution of an object—already defined by a name or perceived by us as such—in order to reach a relationship between two subjects or near subjects as living beings that exist and develop by themselves. The issue which now must be considered by us is that we have previously conceived being as situated in a relationship between a subject and an object and that we lack words to speak of a relationship between two subjects. After having recognized the one that we meet as different from ourselves without reducing this one to an already known through a learned code, are we not speechless before this other? No doubt the relationship exists between us, but we have no word(s) to tell it. In reality, this mode of relationship between the world, the other and ourselves occurred from our infancy, our childhood, and it is inscribed in the depths of us in what is closest to us, but it remains wordless—which paralyses our development and that of our relational life.

Between our original experience of being in relations and its so-called cultural working-out, a continuity has been interrupted so that the modes of meeting which are proposed to us, and even imposed on us, do not ensure the cultivation of the first physical emotions or excitement. Thus these leave in us imprints without any word and act upon our approach to the world and to the other in an unconscious way. To acknowledge what has been taught us and to respect it we are asked to linger again before every being in order to wonder about what or who this being is really in itself and by itself and about the nature of the relationship that we can have with it, even before any articulate language. Henceforth, the matter is no longer one of recognizing what or who appears to us according to the discourse that we have heard about it or them, but of preserving a space for the not-said, not-defined, not-determined in which this other can appear as something or someone that is not yet known or recognized. This exempts us from formatting everything in accordance with information that we have already heard and permits us to open up to a new experience with what or whom we approach. What appears to us in the present is no longer hidden by what has been said about it: we are now facing what is still to be experienced and said. And this compels us to resort to a quite different language which lets the other be without bending it to our saying. A language which lets the presence be without intending to define it a priori. A language which allows any 'to be' to appear independently of our knowledge about it.

To recognize, from then on, means that we do not yet know anything about what or who appears to us, and we must pay attention to and get ready for the disclosure that the meeting can bring to us. This asks us to turn back the way that we have been taught, unlearning words that designate things or people and the manner according to which the totality of the world, especially the world of knowledge, has been constituted. Without indulging in mere criticism—which amounts to remaining in the same horizon—the matter is one of learning how to perceive again, including through our sensory perceptions, what we meet. For example, we have to learn again not to reduce a tree to a mere generic term, but to find time to perceive what it is in the present, a presence that is specific to each individual of its species, but also to each moment of the year, not to say of the day. Identifying, consequently, does not amount to acknowledging or re-cognizing by means of a code but results from the attention that we pay to the presence of the tree here and now—for example, that of a cherry tree in flower in a specific environment—and from welcoming it with our entire being. The meeting with a cherry tree in flower will produce in us a state really different, including at the level of knowledge, from the one occurring after the mention of the word 'cherry tree', to say nothing about the mere word 'tree'.

If we linger a little on contemplating the cherry tree in flower, such contemplation will bring about in us a unification of the various perceptions that have been involved, and will thus constitute us into a whole in connection with another whole, that of the tree. This will exempt us from achieving our unification by composing the world into a totality. The particularity and singularity of each, be it a human or a tree, is now preserved as that of the relationship which links them together. And such particularity is no longer that of objects but of living beings, which are each singular, and between which the relations remain living. This means having access to a really other cultural universe, of which time and space and also the components and their links, as well as their linguistic expression are different and favour evolution instead of maintaining an immutable permanence.

This seems to be impossible for us. However, not to attain this other way of using language amounts to using word(s) as an instrument of death and not of life. And yet we cannot abandon we cannot content ourselves as speaking being with such a destiny. It is thus incumbent on us to give another function to the word, especially as far as living beings are concerned. Instead of designating and apprehending them through a name, we must make room around them to give them a place for their own word. Even outside any articulate language, a tree tells itself and talks to us, and we have to pay attention to this before we intend to speak in its place and by means of knowledge founded above all on vision. In reality, life as such is not seen and the tree as living appears to us only indirectly. Reducing it to an object of our knowledge and our sight amounts to removing it from what it really is.

This is, or ought to be, all the more the case when it is a question of a human. And our culture continually needs to correct its tendency to reduce everything to object(s), especially through moral rules. In reality, these take into account the death of the body but not that of the soul, of the psyche in its whole, and barely that of the spirit. When our logic favours subject–object relations, without being much concerned with discovering and establishing what would be a logic of intersubjectivity, it does not consider breath and energy which enliven the existence of living beings and render them irreducible to objects subjected to a human grasp and assessment. It removes beings from their living conditions and reduces them to inanimate products. However variant the grammar may be, that its category of animate person makes possible, the other, and even oneself, are then subjected to syntactic structures which paralyze the becoming of each and of the relations that each can have with other living beings. Therefore, our way of knowing amounts to acting on and transforming the real instead of saying what or who it is and its relational potential. As Max Planck claims: 'Is real what one can measure'. However it is not the case for what is living.

12

Desire as Rebirth

The other appears as the one he or she is. Their being is revealed if they are capable of dwelling in it—if they know self-affection as a place to inhabit themselves in an autonomous manner. And also if, while withdrawing into themselves, they allow their presence to radiate as an offering of whom and what they are. Such an appearing, to which they agree, is the telling of a closeness to themselves which can be contemplated, acknowledged and welcome. But it cannot be reduced to an immediate experience or a mere object of perception. It must be respected as a closeness which can be perceived thanks to a distance—a distance from oneself and a distance from the other, two distances which cannot be mistaken for one another.

What is received from such closeness radiating into a presence, as its secret silent offering, cannot be simply told or told again through words, unless we take the risk of dispossessing the other, but also ourselves, of it. To perceive here calls for accompanying a becoming without removing it from what permits it to exist. The accompaniment may be of a parental or amorous kind, inspired by a need for help or a desire for sharing.

The ones who really desires us gives us to us, offers us a chance of existing—and, perhaps, of feeling desire for him or for her, if this

© The Author(s) 2017
L. Irigaray, *To Be Born*, DOI 10.1007/978-3-319-39222-6_12

corresponds to their own growth. However, if their desire is real, it aims at what contributes to their being. It is an appeal for a sharing of being so that the latter can arise, appear and blossom in each one, and also between the two. It is as a prayer directed to the other to bring me back to myself while him or her dwelling in themself (cf. Robert and Collins, p. 2038) to whom I am attracted. It is a request for the other to save in themself a place which helps me to remember the one who I am and to be faithful to myself. This allows the other to gather with themself too, without any constitution of an object and, so, to continue being and becoming as a living being. Indeed, the desire for the other is the sap which makes possible such development for a human. Such desire invites us to remember being living.

Desire for the other must be kept in our thinking. In reality, the source of what we have to think about is the desirable. For lack of this source, we no longer move—we no longer live. And what thought can exist without arising from life? Desire for the other reminds us of this elementary truth if we care about what it arouses in ourselves. What must be thought is not only what must be kept in our memory, it is also, and perhaps firstly, what contributes towards our becoming. The other is the one who compels us to become what or who we are not yet. Desire is the premonition of a possible 'not yet' of our being. At least this is the case if desiring does not confine itself to willing, appropriating, owning, consuming. Then desire destroys the surge towards the beyond, which is its most characteristic feature as human. It amounts to a mere instinct or drive determined by an economy extraneous to the achievement of our human being.

Desire is a call for us to unveil what our own being consists of and to discover how to allow it to remain and grow as a being. Neglecting to care about a thought of desire probably results from despising the living and sensitive aspect of our being. Such negligence has rendered our method of thinking inappropriate to a cultivation of desire, which consequently escapes and turns away from our way of imagining, our logic, our language. Desire is absent from our culture and reappears only in its margins, its effects, its flaws.

Such cultural aporia might be mistaken with the withdrawal of the other in themself which awakens our desire as the source or the enigma of the desirable. Only a human being is capable of withdrawing in itself in a manner that is not merely reactive. Withdrawing in themself, the other reminds us of the non-representable nature of our being and of the fact that a human is able to welcome and even give birth to a presence without understanding its mystery but by acknowledging it as irreducible to any grasp. What appeals to us by withdrawing is something or someone to which we can give place and birth, or rebirth. We must resist following this movement of withdrawing in order to respect it, as required by being, especially the being of the other, to preserve it from appearing and so saving its source of becoming.

The desire that we feel for such withdrawing is a desire to be, a longing for being which demands from us also a withdrawing in ourselves. This withdrawal is not nothing, it corresponds to the concern about being that we incarnate. It is an attempt to keep it, to safeguard it from scattering, from vanishing, from being reduced to appearance, from being appropriated. It is an endeavour to maintain being alive, to bring it back to its source so that it can develop, notably while waiting for the capacity of the other to welcome it, to give it a place and sometimes forms. We will have to take these into account as facing ourselves, including an 'ourselves' that the other perceives or conceives in their own way. We must meet it, consider it, without letting it destroy our own being, that is, without letting ourselves be attracted outside the withdrawal and the source which can provide our own being with its living forms. We must assess whether what the other presents to us asks us to leave ourselves or brings us back to ourselves, to our own becoming, thanks to what it gives us to embody, to think, to share, especially about life and its origin.

In our world in which 'the desert is growing' (Nietzsche) and 'the distress spreads', especially because of 'the planning of a uniform happiness for all' (Heidegger), the existence of the other opens a breach in a horizon by which we are weighed down as a shape of lead or a dusk where all becomes grey. Through the desire awakened or revived in us, the other calls us to a beyond—to live and to think the 'not yet'. The other allows us to keep in our memory, in our whole being, the place of a 'not yet' as the hope of a future. This 'not yet' must not be experienced as a void that we have to fill, but as the maintenance in us of an availability to welcome truth, beauty, joy, one could say grace. Which can save us from an eventual despair or melancholy resulting from a nothing for which we can wait, a nothing we can build and become.

Desire upsets our representation of the world in which differences are abolished and what they can question of the model are imposed on us. Desire resurfaces as the source which has structured the whole of our universe, a source that the latter did not take into account and which remains outside of its horizon. Desire reminds us of the non-representable nature of origin: our own, that of the other and of the world. It restores the bond between the within us and the outside of us. It brings us back to a being into presence extraneous to the circle of representation. At least it ought to be so if desire succeeds in not being captured by the current organization of our world—if life preserves a margin of freedom where desire can appear and question such organization, particularly by a return to perception.

Representation anaesthetizes perception, it covers it, forgets about it. Could this be because perception may put it into question? Or shake its legitimacy? Even suspect it of harming? Indeed, can representation contribute to keeping in memory the presence of a living being? If I merely imagine a tree in bloom, what remains of our presence the one to the other? If I only imagine the other, who awakened desire in myself, might I not in this way nullify their presence as life and the origin of my desire—a presence similar to a silence beyond any word? Nevertheless, I hear this presence because it speaks to my being, invites me to be or reminds me of being. It is a draught, a waking up of my heart or my thought in a close and dozed off universe that desert invades. Such a presence is calling me up to my way of becoming myself, firstly by questioning me about what and who I am. It is a question that can be wrongly answered by appropriating or cancelling the other. Rather, the matter is one of recognizing this other as other, and of freeing myself from a lack of differentiation between us so that I can be faithful to myself, each of us dwelling in our own place in order that a meeting between the two can occur.

Desire knows the difference between beings, nevertheless it leaps it over towards what is yet to be. It wants the beyond, a future in search of its revelation and its embodiment. It attempts to discover gestures and words which unveil the way to be made. It overcomes the obstacle of what hinders it before tackling it properly and trying to solve it. Desire moves more quickly than wind, surmounts gravity, has something to do with ether. It has also something in common with the angel who flies towards the other for us uniting with one another before this union being possible. It announces and opens a path that we will have to start along step by step again, taking into account what or who we are now and an incitement to become what or who we are not yet, each one of us and, perhaps, all together.

13

The Necessity of Love

Desire incites us to be, or reminds us of being. By desire we are also compelled to come up to the other's expectation. Desire is a bridge between ourselves and the other, between ourselves and the beyond too, as well as between the past, the present and the future. But how can we answer its call? How can we remember the place where desire summons us? Supposing that we did not lose its tracks, we did not forget it, given that we are divided between a remainder of natural belonging, the cultivation of which has been neglected, and cultural constructions extraneous to our original vitality, the dynamism of which is often invested in idealities which do not contribute towards the blossoming of our flesh. Ought we to continue destroying desire as such by substituting for it instinct or mere vital impetus on the one hand, and God, Good and (at best) Beauty on the other hand? Which makes the carnal meeting between us impossible—we do not exist where it could happen. Hence our distress and dereliction because the attraction between us cannot be embodied. Indeed, desire wants reconciliation of the body and the soul, of the body and the spirit. To desire means longing for uniting a bodily conjunction with what transcends us, for uniting here and now with a beyond, within ourselves and between us.

© The Author(s) 2017
L. Irigaray, *To Be Born*, DOI 10.1007/978-3-319-39222-6_13

Unfortunately, the path to achieve such union is still lacking. We must discover it, invent it, clear it, whereas desire aspires to its immediate fulfillment. Consequently, it wastes energy which it does not know how to deal with, instead of attempting to elaborate it patiently. But how to do this? And how to lead the other to accompany such a persevering approach to the incarnation of desire? How to preserve the awakening of our flesh that desire aroused, to keep alive the surge of energy which compels us to unite with one another, while giving to ourselves the space and time that our global being needs to become capable of fitting them in without destroying ourselves or the other, and so annihilating desire itself?

It is not by chance that the most beautiful legacies of our culture with regard to desire bear witness to the quest to which it gives rise without telling a great deal about the fulfilment of its sharing. Desire gives us back to life, but how can we care for this newborn? Perhaps its unique chance of living and developing is to venture to share love.

Love brings space and time to the other outside of us but also within us in order that what this other entrusts of his or her being to us can live, grow, blossom—which cannot occur with the immediacy and impetuosity of desire. Love grants a silent peace which enables the lightning announcing desire to become an enchantment which no longer attracts outside of oneself but invites to dwell in oneself, to cultivate what has been perceived, received and let it develop up to, but also thanks to, the word that it will generate. Love gives word to what desire has drawn, opened up, cleared, caused. It is love which can give to desire the power to say, to tell itself, while preserving a source of word which, itself, never comes up directly to language. Love watches out for the hardly born, which needs to be safeguarded and assisted in growing and blooming until it appears, dares to manifest itself, and so becomes sign. Love is what renders possible an unsheltering which does not amount to an exiling ecstasis outside of onesel, and it can also lead the awakening of the sensitiveness that desire arouses to a flowering that is likely to be shared. Love can also care about maintaining the sensitive, the carnal, when we pass to the transcendental level that desire requires for our relations being really human. Love is what contributes to uniting in ourselves a physical emotion with a spiritual emotion, to restoring a continuity between our body and our soul or our spirit that our tradition too often has divided. In this way it misjudged the meaning of the amorous union, it reduced it to the relaxation of tensions, to a return to homeostasis, according to Freudian theory, instead of considering it to be a crucial moment in the accomplishment of humanity.

This moment has something to do with what is said between Heidegger and a Japanese master about the unfolding of the word (cf. Martin Heidegger, 'A Dialogue on Language', in *On the Way to Language*, pp. 1–54). It corresponds to the most intimate time of the exchange, to a carnal dialogue, from which the unfolding of the word can take place for and from each and towards which it leads as in a sort of 'hermeneutic circle'. The duality of unfolding and their difference prevent this circle from ever closing up. Indeed, not only must each return to the source of its being, but the amorous union between the two different beings generates also a third being, a fruit of this union, that neither of them can really appropriate, and which remains the most unsayable source of the gathering which rules over the unfolding of the word. Indeed, this origin will remain veiled by the turning back of each to its own presumed origin, even if the latter is also granted by the union between the two. The amorous embrace is an intertwining of two unfoldings of the word, from which being—and even an original 'to be'—is told without its secret being ever will be revealed. Entrusted to the most intimate interlaced touch of two fleshes it belongs to either of them and fulfils the conjunction between their enigmas, the one for the other in a more profound mystery.

It is not by chance that many traditions have represented the origin of the world by a couple, especially a divine or sacred one. It is there that the source, not only of the flesh but also of the word, which is indissociable from it, lies. To divide the one from the other amounts to depriving the body of life and the word of meaning. Only love can keep them united, as much indispensable to the one as to the other, rendering them in a way indissoluble from one another. Only love is the sun which allows desire to develop and appear as gestures or words, like flowers which say the unsayable of being, the holding a dialogue of what is originally silence (cf. the use of the word 'koto-ba' in 'A Dialogue on Language', in *On the Way to Language*, pp. 45–8). Only love is capable of radiance or with-drawal so as to let be that of which desire was the omen, appealing and helping it to become, while preserving space and time for its fulfilment—which requires the impetus of desire to have appeared and its awakening to be maintained.

If desire has something to do with lightning, love is rather like a sunlight which tames the spark, leading it from dawn to midday and then taking it back from the fullness of the day to another night, in which new lightning perhaps will fly out. Love has to deal with the courage and the patience of the experience of fire or of the dazzling light which happens, affects, shakes and transforms us. Love agrees to welcome what touches us, to endure, even to suffer, it by opening up to it, completely exposing ourselves to its awakening until we discover a meaning to attribute to it and the words that are likely to ensure our memory of it so that the sensitive experience can subsist without for all that resorting to an abstract formulation.

Love helps the vibrations of desire, the turbulence of energy and the shaking of the body to gather in a meaningful manner so that they can last and obtain a value and a measure suitable for a human being. Love makes desire become a word which maintains a polyphonic nature, irreducible to the linearity of a wording which would remove it from its carnal belonging.

Love acts as a sort of grace which transforms the instinctive strength of attraction into a radiating flesh, which regains a porousness that renders it capable of being in communion with an other. It has recovered the radiant gathering itself together of a living being, the flesh of which, stimulated by warmth and light, blooms into forms, and even overflows them while being capable of restraint towards the other. It, itself, becomes sign in the name of desire of which it expresses the welcome and appeal—a sign in which matter and form interact, thwarting the logic that rules over our conception of meaning.

In order that such an advent can happen, love has to bring to the lightning of desire the slackening and spreading out that only trust can grant, the abandon to confidence in agreeing to give up willing all by and for oneself and the hope for a future still to come. Giving up reaching everything straightway corresponds to a renunciation which opens up the possibility of a coming or a growing which cannot be foreseen, but which we must let be, even when no word yet exists.

It is in such a flaw that the amorous union takes place as the experience of an original saying to which we have to give and give again birth. No doubt, such a site has to be made possible by preliminaries, through gesturing words which prepare, preserve and safeguard the place of a not-yet in which to venture—gesturing words which call, welcome, take part, agree to closeness, to intimacy with what it involves of unknowable, of non-appropriable, of absence and anguish. It is in an active way that we must prepare for having access to the not-yet from which an 'it is' or 'to be' can arise, conceived by the union between two different beings—origin of a new word. It is there that it can and must occur in a meeting between two fleshes, two worlds, two discourses. By separating the word from the body, the verb from the flesh, the one presupposed to be of divine nature and the other of human nature, our tradition prevented such an advent from happening. Indeed, it is their indissociable connection and interaction in each of us that allows us, through the risk of their coming into presence between us as different, to give rise to a new word likely to contribute towards the becoming of a new humanity—one could say of humanity as such.

It is between us that the advent of the verb becoming flesh and the flesh becoming verb must take place. To entrust the word and its incarnation only to God or an exclusively spiritual absolute, leaves us, as humans, carnally fallen or decayed and constrained to aspire to such transcendences in order to endeavour to redeem ourselves with the eventuality of then incarnating our terrestrial existence—which makes impossible our carnal union becoming the place from which the unfolding of the word springs and to which it returns after its various embodiments by each. Now what or who is a human being if it is not the place from which the word can arise? And what happens with humanity if man claims he, alone, to hold the source of the word without acknowledging that it springs from the conjunction between the man and the woman? Which amounts to entrusting to their union the concern for being itself, the origin of which always conceals itself from appearing, but which must be preserved as the place of its non-appropriable withdrawing and arising between those who love one another.

14

Giving Birth to One Another

If 'questioning is the piety of thinking' and if 'the passion of knowing is to question' (cf. Heidegger, 'The nature of language', in *On the Way of Language*, p. 72, and *Introduction to Metaphysics,* p. 171), then desire is what most corresponds to it. Desire touches us, moves us, awakes our interest, questions us about our being, in a way that orders us to pay attention to it. The problem which faces us is that we lack some method with regard to it, we do not know how to make our way with it, in it. If our culture accustomed us to reduce everything to the same—even to the Same—we are henceforth compelled to take difference into account. This means that we constantly must follow our path in the opening of a 'not that', 'not there', 'not yet', 'not knowable', 'not appropriable' and so on. Clearing our way must always take into consideration the negative, including concerning what we feel or experience and not only what lies outside of us. While advancing, we must continuously make room, not only before ourselves, not only for imagining or representing what appears to us—as our tradition has taught us—but also within ourselves—what our logic did not teach us. We have thus to invent the path, and invent it together.

© The Author(s) 2017
L. Irigaray, *To Be Born*, DOI 10.1007/978-3-319-39222-6_14

Desire which attracts us, which enjoins us to approach, to unite with one another, in reality is like a word. We do not know the meaning of this word apart from that of an emotion, an appeal. In order to go further than a mere sensitive immediacy, perhaps we could first listen to the 'tone' of the call. We then realize that the tonality of desire varies according to those between whom it arises. Before any articulate word, the experience of desire does not lack differentiation. It conveys a signification that we have to decipher in order to hear it, cultivate it, share it—on this side of, or beyond, any term. Before we can utter any word, being in harmony with the desire that we perceive corresponds to an original mode of saying. Already we confide to the other, in the other, to whom we are so telling while listening to him or to her.

Desire takes place when and where listening to and talking to are inextricably linked and we reveal ourselves as fleshes which are telling to one another. We commit the other what we have of most intimate without being really conscious of what we are telling. We become engaged to one another almost without our knowing, but with a commitment of our being more radical than any articulate language can grant us. We give to one another our word without even knowing what word we then commit. Hence the difficulty, even the distress, when this word is called into question while we bond ourselves in an absolute way. Nevertheless it needs to be done, because if our attraction, our approach and our union are not a source of word, they will sink into a nothing of being and thus give rise to an anguish and a dereliction still more radical. We must remain faithful while freeing ourselves from the immediacy of our commitment—to continue pledging our word to one another the time to experience if our beings, our 'to be', could become consonant and can be in harmony towards a being together at the origin of an additional being for each and the world where we live.

The path of desire is probably the most difficult to conceive, to go. It is also probably the most religious. Fortunately, the awakening of desire is accompanied by enthusiasm that brings to our habitual breath additional ardour and joy, which allows us to achieve an undertaking exceeding the accomplishment of our own existence: a sharing and generating of life itself.

However, enthusiasm urges us to do more than merely letting happen, and to create more than simply communing with ourselves and being attentive to one another. Now desire asks us to listen to and receive what is confided. It requires a letting be said as much as a saying. And this necessitates our preserving a place in which this can happen. Enthusiasm, which induces us to leave ourselves in order to behave with an almost divine ardour, has to be curbed, to withdraw into or turn in on ourselves (cf. dictionary: se replier) in order to make room for welcoming and listening to. Enthusiasm must not merely pour thoughtlessly but collect itself in order to prepare for sharing. It has to listen instead of unfurling in saying, what may be the modes of the latter. It must put telling of desire to the test until it becomes an experience of desire which leads each to find its own word. Telling desire to one another is necessary in order to discover the tone that can be shared, and to sing it together. Song corresponds more to a common talking of desire which, though being the source of the word, remains itself unspeakable. What each brings to the other through desire has to be a return to the source—a rebirth—which grants him or her, but also enjoins them, to renew with their origin in order to become, starting from it again, and from an energy that takes root in nature and is shareable as such.

This permits us to unite with one another in the enthusiasm that desire arouses instead of in the complicity resulting from a subjection to the same ideals imposed on us. Only in the first case does what is confided in us by desire call us to the origin of the word, question the relations between to be and to say. Such questioning is likely to unveil what the meaning of our mutual attraction is beyond the harmony of tones. It wonders whether desire can develop, whether it opens out onto a future which is founded both in nature and in word(s), which amounts to saying that it is founded in a human way. This questioning inquires about attraction for one another, about the closeness it can provoke. Will it be able to go from a juxtaposition or a face-to-face meeting to an intimacy in which the two interlace until, sometimes, they merge, and anyway are present to one another beyond any representation? This needs another logic and another word which take root in the, partly blind, attraction for one another as different. The path is then more inspired and paved by listening and touch than by watchful eyes. It is on this side and beyond anything visible that desire calls for joining one another cf. dictionary, p. 523) with trial and error in which the mystery of the origin and the night of the prenatal attempt to renew with the most achieved of human being.

It seems that nothing urges the one to unite with the other, but longing exists which, sometimes, appears to prevail over the force of gravity itself. Elation also results from the fact that heaviness is no longer perceived, each feeling itself being carried towards, but also by, the other, as it happens at the beginning of existence. No one still dwells in oneself, and it is little by little that one must return to oneself, in oneself.

Nevertheless, this new birth is different from the first, even if it may arouse in us some nostalgia for regressing to the most original of our life, of its environment and of the human assistance that we received because of our physical immaturity. However, even if our culture maintained us in a state of immaturity with regard to sharing desire, the situation is no longer the same. And turning back to primitive needs runs the risk of destroying the fire of desire, the aim of which is to transcend what already exists and not to regress to a subjection due to the requirements of a mere survival. Desire requires ascending and not falling, and it is not by chance that our tradition kept it in abeyance through absolutes and ideals that are out of our reach here below.

But this is not what desire wants. It longs to transcend our solitary incarnation, to attain here and now another existence in which the awakening and sharing of an energy, both physical and spiritual, allow us to enter together into another terrestrial life. We lack word(s) for such an event or advent in which our saying has its origin.

Experiencing the relation between our two different beings remains largely neglected in our culture. Hence the fact of reducing our amorous attraction to a mere instinct, including an instinct of procreation. The most transcendental of our aspirations is so limited to the most unthought of our natural belonging: an appeal existing between two living beings differently sexuate. And this relation is all the more unthinkable since the intimate touch is what acts as a guide as far as it is concerned. Consequently, the parameters which rule over our traditional logic—visibility, face to face or representation—are no longer really helpful, and it is the way of getting in touch itself which remains inconceivable, and not only the relation as such. Urged to unite with one

another, those who desire nevertheless remain parted—one and one—
what is more without mutual knowing, and their want of one another as
unknowable lacks an imaginable path to be taken.

The link to be formed, the most desirable by our humanity, is
unattainable, except by chance or thanks to a persevering listening to
our tactile perceptions. But to harmonize in ourselves and between us
what we perceive through our body, our psyche and our mind is not an
easy task. The matter is thus not only of finding a syntax suitable for
overcoming the parataxis of our different identities, but also of discovering a way of uniting in ourselves dimensions or aspects that our culture
has kept separate. This calls for a transformation of our natural energy,
of our physical energy, so that our body can become the mediator of the
union between us rather than a material obstacle intervening between
the one and the other. Our body must become a bridge, in us and
between us, ensuring the passage from a past humanity to a new
humanity—from the old man of the West to the one that Nietzsche
wrongly called a superman—for which it is from then on relation itself
which is the source of the word, more than the terms between which a
connexion is yet to be established.

Criticizing and abandoning the suprasensitive values, thanks to
which humanity kept its becoming on hold, forces us to discover
another setting or frame starting from which we can achieve our
destiny. Our sexuate identity seems to be able to act in this way. Our
physical, psychic and mental or spiritual sexuation provides us with a
frame capable of shaping our living energy so that we have no longer to
project it outside of ourselves, exiled in this way from a destiny that we
attempt to get back as a distant horizon which addresses us with
enigmatic signs. Moreover, such a destiny does not only divide us
from ourselves but also separates us from one another because it is
determined by our sexuate belonging in an unconscious, thus not
shareable, way. In this destiny our sexuate identity is objectivized and
we are thus deprived of it subjectively.

We can return our sexuate destiny to one another, we can give back to
each other this donation of our birth, not as a mere anatomic fate—
according to the words of Freud—but as a destiny which concerns being
itself, which can especially happen thanks to a desire and a love that are

respectful of our mutual difference(s). Then our sexuation sends us back to our natural origin, provides us not only with the surge which brings us towards one another and the restraint which invites us to remain in ourselves, but also procures us a structure for entering into relations between ourselves. In Heideggerian terms one could say that it acts as the *Gestell* towards the *ereignis* of our human being, which at once belongs and does not belong to each of us.

These relations now go further than a sensitive or sensual dependence and subordination or a lack of differentiation. Sensitivity, including the bodily one, becomes that which contributes to our individuation thanks to its sexuate specificity. No doubt this does not occur without distress and even pain due to the insuperable distance in nearness, distance from oneself and from the other. To be human asks us to become capable of assuming the dereliction and distress—as Heidegger, after Victor Hugo or with René Char, would say—of the impossible appropriation of desire, of sheltering in ourselves and between ourselves a nothing that no unity can overcome. To consider seriously our sexuation corresponds to the turning point—the *Kehre, according to* Heidegger—which inserts, or inserts again, our to be into being, as the sap of a transcendence of which we must take care, especially for each other, without abandoning it to ideals or absolutes beyond our reach.

15

To Conceive a New World

There is no doubt that a certain epoch of our culture is coming to an end: that of our past metaphysics which finally came to be embodied in the scientific and technical era which is henceforth ours. Indeed, either humanity and the world in which it dwells are disappearing or we discover a way of turning or returning to what being a human means in order to think out it as the first actor on our destiny and about the possibility of attaining a word which technique and technologies cannot deprive us of by reducing us to sorts of mechanisms of a less high-performance than those we can produce.

It is in ourselves as incarnate human beings that we can find a new way of thinking about how to escape the domination by technique and technologies without underrating their merit. By inviting us to free ourselves from subjection to suprasensive ideals, Nietzsche in part tells us to which direction we must turn. But his teaching is above all a critical one, and the one that inspired the deconstruction of Western metaphysics carried out, after him, by Heidegger and his followers. If Nietzsche has rightly intuited that we have to make a fresh beginning, especially by starting from our physical belonging again in order to pass from the old man of the West to a new humanity, he lacked the time to clear the path or build the bridge to achieve this aim. I am afraid that even the 'will to power' and 'the eternal

© The Author(s) 2017
L. Irigaray, *To Be Born*, DOI 10.1007/978-3-319-39222-6_15

return' somehow or other remain in the horizon of our past logic. They act as instruments of its interpretation, they procure a perspective which allows us to free ourselves from it. But the inspired intuitions of Nietzsche, as Heidegger calls them, do not provide us with the frame that we need to build a culture which fits our incarnation.

This frame—which Heidegger sometimes calls 'inspection'—which makes possible the advent of a new epoch of truth and culture, must, henceforth, lie in our body, as a structure which is proper to it and through which it can say itself anew as far as the world and all the elements which have a part in it are concerned. Such a structure exists and already expresses itself, even in an unconscious way, in our past conception of the real and of the language which tells it—it corresponds to the sexuation of our identity. In what has been called human being, an aspect which determines the nature of this being has remained ignored, an aspect which contributes to taking it away from a disembodied neutrality, which does not allow human being to appear as it is, and which resurfaces in spite of a presumed truth of the world and of the things which does not correspond to it.

The peril that the neutralization of a humans as a living beings represents is becoming manifest today through the development into robots of various elements of the world, through its organization from the potential of mechanisms that the human mind has produced, but of which it has become the servant, exiled from its living belonging. Whatever their performative potential, human beings have already exceeded by that of the machine on several levels. Their salvation can only come from the perception of the peril and the manner of overcoming it, while attaching meaning to it, and through a return to their own being as specific living beings. In order to go beyond a conception of the world that a technical way of thinking and behaving governs, we must discover another frame or structure thanks to which the human beings may escape such domination while acknowledging and interpreting the nature of its power. We must free ourselves from the technical and scientific ascendance over our epoch and ensure the safeguarding of meaning by a new incarnation of being.

In reality, the meaning that we must consider and cultivate in our epoch is first that of life itself. Life obviously is in danger, and how could we intend to be if we are no longer living? We have thus to turn back the path taken by our culture in order to understand when and how it has failed in cultivating life. No doubt the task of Greek thinkers was to secure a deal with an extra life by supplying it with links and gathering it into a whole—in some way as a gardener cares about the garden of which he is in charge. But our task is no longer that of the Greeks: we suffer from a lack of life, and not from extra life. The structures with which we have mastered the living world have little by little exhausted its sap and we are now suffering from a shortage rather than from a surplus of vigour. Hence the necessity of attending to the preservation, not so much of a being—or Being—beyond living, but to what permits life itself to exist. It is about the energy potential which sustains life that we must now care about, and not about exuberant excesses of growth. We must recover the energy that we kept in abeyance through suprasensitive ideals or that we delegated to machines if we do not want life to vanish. And before being watchful of any language already articulate, we must be careful to cultivate our breathing and our desire. We must free them from forms and links in which they have been invested and are held so that, after liberating their energy potential, we may discover the modes likely to save and increase it, especially thanks to a sharing with other living beings.

This reawakening of life, this questioning about the way in which we have used our energy, can result from the spark flying out in a meeting between two human beings. In his text devoted to 'The End of Philosophy and the Turning Point', Heidegger explains how the spark, lit in the depth of things, is what can provoke a turnaround in thinking and bring back being to what is more proper to it than what it already developed of its 'to be'. In Western philosophy, Heidegger entrusts to our sight the task of lighting the spark. No doubt, he says on several occasions that looking at, for him, does not relate only to sight strictly speaking. Nevertheless, his comments on the spark which leads our being to turn to what it more essentially is correspond generally to visual features and presuppose a reference to one subject only. It is surprising that Heidegger—whose amorous relations have represented an appreciable part his existence—does not imagine that the spark can fly out from the meeting between two human beings, as precisely that which is called falling in love as quick as a flash. Now this shakes our way of incarnating our 'to be' and is likely to introduce us to a new stage of our incarnation. Of course this happens only if we pay attention to what then takes place, instead of wasting it in agitation and the spending of energy, which aim at destroying it without questioning its meaning.

Then we are no longer the ones who look at, even at an inner being, but the ones who are touched in ourselves by the other, and who welcome what is perceived, beyond all what has been previously experienced, and is perceptible only by us. The spark, which provokes in us an awakening or reawakening of our being, apart from the fact that it invites us to take another path, to adopt another method, in order to answer it, also plunges us into uncertainty with regard to what belongs to each of us. Indeed, the spark lights in a meeting between two beings and this occurrence escapes not only any appropriation but also any provenance from or convenience to anyone.

About it we can only say 'it is', and to take care of this 'it is' compels us to enter into a new epoch of thought and history in which the relation between two beings, especially two human beings who are naturally different, is the place where our 'to be' shelters and withdraws. And this does not happen without endangering this 'to be' and ourselves in a quite different manner from that resulting from technique and technology. The spark that the awakening of our desire lights in us brings back into the depths of our intimacy that which we projected in the distance. If our being is in this way brought back to its source, we are without the means to master and even preserve it. We have failed to cultivate life itself and what constitutes its sap, and we are thus sent back to the most obscure enigma of this aporia. If we are now more alive and bursting with energy, we are also plunged into night. We have not learned that touch itself can become light. We have no beacon, no word, to orient ourselves.

Moreover, the path is no longer to be cleared by one alone. We are in search of it, the one and the other, the one towards the other, and touch is our guide—a touch which is mysteriously closer to us than any proximity, but in which the other takes place. It is no longer 'there' that we have to deal with him or her but in the most secret of our 'here'. And such an advent may either send us back to the origin of our being or annihilate it. At least it may remove us even more from it, according to whether we are or are not capable of keeping and making shine what has been entrusted to us on this side or beyond any knowledge, if not the perception of a sharing of life, which has left us without sight or voice and yet more bright than ever.

How can we acknowledge and cultivate the fact that being happens to our sharing? How can we accept that being can unfold, Heidegger would ask, or that it can arise from between us? Truth then takes another shape and is endowed with another sort of light, be it that of the world or of any being which composes it. What is more, such shaping and light place not only natural energy at our disposal but they also produce natural energy in each of us and between us. This natural donation becomes the origin of a new mode of being in relation to the sort of relating to one another that the difference of sexuate identities requires. Instead of transforming it into a mechanical one, we bring the natural energy of such a donation to its production and increase it whilst it remains natural. This calls for our will not only to be in accordance with this energy in us, but also to be a good match with that of the other. Obviously this requires the 'to be' and the being of the woman not to be at the man's disposal, but for a fertilizing meeting to occur between two different 'to be's and beings.

We must venture to experience what then happens in order to reach this potential of being—and not only at the level of thinking, as Heidegger seems to suggest. Such a risk, nevertheless, remains faithful to our becoming between nature and culture, earth and heaven, humanity and divinity. It does not amount to the peril that a technological universe represents when putting our natural belonging at the disposal of a framework—a *Gestell*—which consumes its energy instead of transforming it in a way which makes it more suitable for us.

Now we risk welcoming the world of the other into the depths of our intimacy. But what is most extraneous to us is, in this case, what corresponds to the greatest closeness, in the sense that the call to the other as different is aroused from what is most original in our being. However, we do not listen to it, we do not pay attention to it, we nullify it through a behaving which lacks thinking. Where word ought to have its most irreducible site—between us as different living beings—we obliterate the place of its possible springing and are unfaithful to our destiny which asks us to give meaning to the real that we are. We impose on this real representations which are presumed to contribute to its preservation and its entering into presence, but which in fact cut it off from its source and its becoming. Instead of the call to and from the other being at the origin of what allows this other, and also us, to provide ourselves with a human face, we ascribe to the other a sort of mask resulting from our representation(s), a mask which paralyses their flowering, and also ours.

Life can exist and develop only from an unrepresented. And to let the human face blossom from desire and love, especially those inspired by life, ends by changing the face of the world in which we live so that it becomes a place in which living beings can dwell and coexist. Henceforth, the world is based on life and its cultivation, and not only on representation(s) that we can have of it.

There is no doubt that between life and ourselves a discontinuity must be established, but it must above all result from the respect for the irreducible difference between living beings, which lets each be what or who it is, and not from the mastery of the entering into presence of every living being through representation(s). Any being must be entrusted to the one that it really is in order that its staying amongst others can take place. It is thanks to faithfulness to what or who each is and a communication or communion with others as others that the face of a world built from life and its development can appear by itself, a face that we can only contemplate while cultivating the life that we, ourselves, are and by sharing what can be shared of it towards its growth and its generation.

To be faithful to life is possible if we pay attention to it and ensure its manifestation and memory, whereas any other faithfulness needs constructed frameworks which paralyse it. Our body remembers, and above all that of the other which has touched it. It is on such a memory that we can found the world again by discovering a way of thinking and saying such a constellation of our 'to be', and its development and its sharing—a 'to be' that has been brought back to life.

16

Bringing Forth the Future

What structured our view and experience of the world for centuries is Western metaphysics. Values which prevailed under its way of conceiving truth and under its rule are suprasensitive ones—Platonic ideas or the God of the Judaeo-Christian tradition—the existence of which result from a technical approach imposed on the real by our logic, our logos. Our philosophy and our monotheistic religions—in other words our onto-theological tradition—have substituted a celestial genealogy for natural roots, that is, a genealogy which somehow or other amounts to the projection onto the beyond of that which our culture prevented us from living here and now. The gathering of ourselves and of the world were structured from presumed universal absolutes extraneous to this absolute that life is, an absolute which then occurs as the unfolding of life in its singularity.

Gathering together of the self and that of the world are today subjected to a technical-scientific control which seems to be the opposite of metaphysics but which, in fact, amounts to its logical accomplishment. The framework which favoured the development of the cultural horizon of metaphysics is in reality a technical one. And it is understandable that this framework appears as such when metaphysics reaches

© The Author(s) 2017
L. Irigaray, *To Be Born*, DOI 10.1007/978-3-319-39222-6_16

the end of its unfolding. The technical-scientific structure, which underpinned our metaphysical tradition, reveals itself henceforth in a privileged way as the cybernetics which plans and organizes the human behaviours and activities of the social milieu (cf. Heidegger, *Introduction to Metaphysics, Chapter IV, 2*, pp. 113–14). Then language becomes a tool of use for informing, and its meaning is determined by representation, evaluation and calculation.

If the potential, especially the transcendental potential, of the child has been subjected to the universe of needs because of its initial immaturity, ours is now destroyed by a culture which transforms us into people cared for by technical power and technologies, by a world that we little by little have created but which henceforth dominates us. In the two cases, some necessities, especially for the transcendental, of the human as a living being have been neglected. As did the adults and the milieu of our infancy and childhood, the world that we have built deprives us of our real potential. They both take our breath and our wings away, and so prevent us from accomplishing our humanity. We must discover how it is possible for us to found another world. And it is not by merely destroying the world built in a past epoch of history that we can construct the world more suitable for a cultivation of life that we are in need of today, but rather by returning to the origin of our natural identity. We can never reach this origin, and what we believe we grasp of it is always already a substitute for the elusive reality that it will remain for us. Nevertheless, it is from it that we must try to start again. Entering into relations with an other who is different to ourselves by nature gives us a chance of succeeding in this. Instead of destroying the world which already exists, we can elaborate another world thanks to the place that is opened up between us by the respect for our natural difference(s). It is there that life can find, or find again, a background for its cultivation from a genesis in which the body and word fertilize one another in a generation at once determined, infinite and potentially universal. The setting which allows such an advent to occur does not require as a priority us to remove what already exists but to become completely what or who we are, so that our differences, and firstly the sexuate one which belongs to our natural identity, make room for the nothing in common between us from which a sharing can exist and manifest itself without belonging to the one or to the other. The matter is thus less one of destroying than of letting exist the part of our being that has not yet been taken into consideration and which participates, in an irreducible but still unrecognized way, in our subjectivity at an individual, especially relational thus potentially collective, level. It is by acknowledging the impossible reduction of the one to the other and the substitution of the one for the other that we can each develop and generate a new world, starting from the respect for our difference(s).

It is there that a space can be opened or reopened for the occurrence of a new appearing, a new coming into presence of every being. It is there that the clearing—the *Lichtung*—where a new truth can arise and begin unfolding into, a world, can be opened. It is there that meaning of the human 'to be' and of its potential, including the relational and generative one, can meet their word and their thought, due to the perspective and the distance that our sexuate belonging offers in relation to a mere adhering to nature. Thanks to it, we can reveal ourselves, the one to the other, and provide one another with a place in which we can come into presence in the gathering together of our being, so that we let it be perceived and thought, not only by ourselves but also by the other, towards a telling that is still unheard: that which says to us who we are. In this way, we can attain a relation to the world that is more true and perceptive, and less darkened by the projection of what we do not know of ourselves.

The opening necessary for us to think and say ourselves can be obtained, if it is wanted by us, through the respect for sexuate difference which operates a discontinuity, a break, a void in the natural continuum. Unless we close it up by the immediate satisfaction of our attraction, the gap that our respective sexuate belonging opens between us raises to a transcendental status both our natural identity and the relationship between our different natural identities. Only in the space opened between us, due to the call of their conjunction of different fleshes and word(s), can each appear as being what or who he or she is. Only there is the opportunity of being, revealed in their own 'to be', granted the one and the other. The already there of the one and the other—one could say their respective *Dasein*—reopens in the already there of the world a nothing-yet, which gives place and (re)birth to the 'to be' of the one and the other, and to the chance of their future relationship. Only there can we really enter into presence.

If by our natural birth we are abandoned to the natural or constructed world, if we are left to the dereliction due to the break of contiguity with our maternal origin, the place which is opened between us by a mutual desire and love that are respectful of our difference grants us the solitude of a presence which allows us to rediscover our 'to be' and to make it blossom thanks to the trust received from or given to the other. In the fitting out and setting up of such a place, what was the dread of coming alone into the world becomes an acknowledgement and a gift of solitude, which the safeguarding of our incarnation and the sharing of our 'to be' require.

Interweaving our desires, consenting to the work on love and the abandonment to love, creates a place for a new birth, and a possible perpetual rebirth, which now corresponds to a presence to ourselves and to the other—appearing of an incarnation in which body and soul generate one another. This asks us to be capable of withdrawing in ourselves. The place of this withdrawal and the one from which we will appear again, especially to the other, is the depth of the flesh, especially as enlivened by our heart. In order that such a presence can happen in the present, we must be able to commune with ourselves in the most inner recess, in faithfulness to the darkness of our origin.

Our coming into presence also results from our fertilization by a word born of the desire of the other and which calls for a manifestation of desire in return. In order that this can arise, a fleshly heart is needed as mediation between the most physical and the most psychical of our being, which provides earth and blood for the germination of signs which will tell of a possible union. For it to be achieved, a place must be set, a sort of clearing of innocence where the not yet happened can be welcomed, heard, and in which it can germinate from a virgin space continuously won back. In this way, our flesh, our being, become revived and fertilized towards a new blossoming.

The technical-scientific rationalization that henceforth governs our world is concerned with a form of being that we have produced, without it taking really into account our whole 'to be'. It makes us thirsty, exhausts us and lets us, once more, cut ourselves off from the resources of life and transcendence. Somehow or other it substitutes for the parents or masters who have ruled our existence according to our physical immaturity. Such culture still reduces us to our needs but without consideration for our desires and our energetic and creative potential.

It is used as an argument that the structure of such culture is in accordance with that of reason itself. However, would it not be more rational to generate a world which can develop without exhausting our resources of life but by cultivating them, instead of putting our vital reserves at the disposal of the technical-scientific machinery that intends to subject all existence on a world scale? This calls for rebuilding the world, starting from the clearing opened by a meeting of desires between two incarnate beings, respectful of their mutual difference(s). What can act as mediation for cementing such construction is the quality of energy which urges us to unite with one another and not an order defined by the wish to dominate of only one—be this a subject or an absolute—or the necessity of maintaining a minimum of cohesion between the members of a society. In fact, we have projected what can ensure the unity of our being onto an outside of ourselves: a future, a horizon or the totality of a world extraneous to our own 'to be'. From these projections, what Heidegger designates as a constellation of being—of Being(?)—has been formed in which we became invested without being able to really distinguish ourselves from it. Hence, our being was in need of gradually broadening our projections, in space and in time, in search of ourselves.

Desire can realize the unity of our being of which our projections deprive us. And the cultivation of desire between us is the crucible where this unity can be preserved and developed—the preliminary condition for building a new world. For such an advent, what we projected in the furthest distance must return to the most close, not as a spatial juxta-position or a face-to-face but as a potential lying in the most intimate of our flesh, seeking for a word permitting and favouring its growing and blossoming, both individual and relational. This cannot happen without the secret and the depth of a mutual touch that love must take into its care.

To safeguard one another at the source of being is probably the way which can allow a new humanity to emerge and develop. Being, then, must be kept in the one and in the other, by the one and by the other, so that the union between the irreducible singularities of their presences can generate a human 'to be'. This 'to be' is no longer a mysterious and evanescent entity—a sort of neutral Being—extrapolated from the union between us. This 'to be' is an acting or wording of the unity that sometimes we succeed in forming, the saying of a union through which the one and the other give birth to a human being.

Epilogue: On Feet of Dove

I can imagine the scepticism of most people faced with the suggestion of rebuilding the world from a relationship of desire and love between a man and a woman. Nevertheless it is in this place that many myths of origin situate the beginning of the world and that the Apocalypse according to St John lets foresee a propitious happening after the terrible trials that humanity must endure to overcome its subjection to instincts and passions. It is also between the god Siva and his partner—Parvati or Kali—that the alternative between a creative or a destructive evolution of the world is to be decided. And it is there too that the future of humanity is generated.

However, this beginning seems never to have had a suitable unfolding; and whatever has been substituted for it appears incapable of providing humanity with a lasting and happy becoming. Our religious, cultural and political ideals are unable either to secure the safety of humanity or to offer it a plan for constructing a future which corresponds to our current necessities. If God is, in our time, the reason for fatal conflicts between different traditions, the theories and practices which pretend to do without Him do not meet the challenge that we are facing. For example, whatever its presumed (Is: opposition to idealism, materialism concerns a level of our

© The Author(s) 2017
L. Irigaray, *To Be Born*, DOI 10.1007/978-3-319-39222-6

being or existence which already corresponds to a superstructure—if I resort to one of its key words—in relation to this infrastructure that our material, especially our sexuate, belonging is. Given the danger which we are in now it is at another level of interpretation and action that we must intervene. It is life itself which must become the unconditional issue of our decisions and not suprasensitive absolutes that too often are the result of our inability to live. It is life which must become this transhistorical dimension in our perception of space and time so that we can go back to an earlier origin starting from which we may conceive another mode of being.

How can we care about the way? This develops into a configuration of being different for a man or a woman. Their union is the place of a perpetual giving birth to human being from the meeting between two breaths, two desires, two fleshes, two words. Where nothing was between them, if not air, from their attraction and their ability to take on the negative of their difference, the germ of a new human and of a world in which we can really dwell springs up.

As I recalled in the Prologue, Love, according to the testimony of Phaedrus in Plato's *Symposium*, is the most ancient of the gods. Love has no parents and is always in search of a conjunction in which it could become incarnate. Perhaps we could invite Love to take part in our embraces? In this way, Love could dwell between us, amongst all of us. Love could participate in the copula, ending in the generation of new humans and of what binds them together.

In the same dialogue by Plato, Diotima, according to the discourse of Socrates, reminds us of the quest of our amorous desires as a longing for immortality, not only by the procreation of children but through a fecundity of our soul, a creation that can the cause of communal links more powerful than the ties which bind natural parents and children, because the children who are then generated are more beautiful and are immortal. Some aspects are worth adding to the teaching of Diotima regarding love. According to the words of Diotima, the body and the soul remain separate in love, and we have to pass gradually from the love of bodies to the love of souls without any divine could be really contemplated in a transfigured body. When she talks of love, Diotima—as is the case for Phaedrus—resorts to a logical subject–object, lover–loved. She does not consider what happens between two subjects who are both loving, and loved by, one another. Now such love needs the union of the body and the soul in each and between the two. The matter is no longer one of passing from a more material object to a more spiritual object, but of little by little transforming the nature of attraction itself: from the more physical to the more spiritual, from the more individual to the more shared. From Diotima's viewpoint, love is not really shared. And, without doubt, if sharing would happen, it would be the place of the advent of beauty and wisdom, not because these ought to find their definitive and unique form in such an occurrence, but because it is there and from such a union that they have their origin. It is their potential that is immortal by combining that of our sexuate chromosomes with that of our most subtle desire and love, in the respect for our difference of beings.

This requires a thing which Diotima did not think about: the most achieved becoming does not occur when passing from the one to the multiple, towards a presumed more perfect and unique longing, but by transforming longing between those who share amorous desire. The awakening of energy then has not to be suspended in some ideal entity, it, itself, changes and becomes more subtle while remaining fleshly, capable of giving rise to a being in which soul or spirit are not separate from the body but correspond to its flowering.

Human being now is conceived differently. It is no longer relevant to oppose 'to be' and 'to become', because the blossoming of being requires its becoming. It also needs its fleshly sharing and transformation, instead of a subjection to absolutes presupposed to be merely spiritual. The uniqueness of such absolutes, objects for which the lovers long in Diotima's discourse, becomes incarnate in the uniqueness of those who love one another, and the attention which is paid to the most accomplished becoming of the subject is substituted for the emphasis put on the perfection of the object. It would be more appropriate to say 'becoming of the subjects' because the development henceforth takes place between subjects, not between a subject and an object. And what acts as mediation between subjects, who are naturally different, is desire.

Heidegger asserts that the task which is now incumbent on us is to combine love and thought, thought and love. He indicates to us how the link between to be and to love is crucial, though it has been largely ignored by our metaphysical tradition. The connection between our 'to be' and love is what can open up a horizon beyond our traditional conception of being. Henceforth it is in the interlacing of our bodies talking to one another that the transcendental matter, from which our 'to be' takes shape, lies.

Such an *ereignis* leads us to attain what most truly corresponds to our own 'to be' through an experience in which our *Dasein*—our being-there—is determined by our desire and our love and their sharing in difference. Instead of being projected in the distance as a longing in search of its 'object', desire now returns to the self, within the self. In such a turn of the projection towards its source, what our 'to be' can mean is unfolded to us, and we are invited to take care of it in order to be able to share it with the other. Opening our being to the other is, in this way, what forces us to go back to what is most proper to us so that we ensure its safeguard and its development. This perpetual return to us, in ourselves as humans both living and sexuate, means that we can, thanks to a longing love, give rise to a constellation of being which is basically transhistorical and provides being with a permanence, an immortality which has more to do with a constant generation, the origin of which is in our nature, than with an immutable essence.

The incarnation of being as generated by love is expressed in various ways, which go from our most intimate flesh to the most sublime of the divine, passing through the cultural and the political. Already in the *Symposium*, the words of the participants enumerate the moral and civil virtues of love and its essential contribution to the constitution of a state, and even of an army. Those who love are said to be the most capable of conquering because their valour surpasses that of Ares, the god of war. Love is more courageous than him, and it is also more wise, always clearing the way between ignorance and wisdom, without fixing on a single objective, and caring about the being of each one. Love knows that truth does not exist once and for all, but that it is proved by the fecundity of what it produces towards a cultivation of life for all living beings.

Indeed, in an amorous union, not only do the one and the other generate a being common to both, but also to a being which underlies each of their intentions and actions. The copula which happens through their union in difference generates, little by little, the structure—the *Gestell*—which supports the fulfilment of the incarnation of a living world, always in becoming. The advent of our 'to be', also as a gift, occurs thanks to the love of those whom one desires. Such love grants them a power-to-be, assists them in being, while letting be an unfolding proper to them. It offers to each the quiet strength of the loving power towards the achievement of their own potential.

Technical power compensates for the loss of being we are facing. However, it gradually subdues our subjectivities by setting every being in an unconditional and partial objectivity. Language, then, is only a tool for exchanges which lack differentiation at the subjective level, and it contributes towards the robotization of humans, whom it no longer can ensure the safety of.

We must give back a source to the word, in us and between us, through a relational behaviour which takes root in our flesh. In such a configuration, each claims the right to be in the other and from the other. Love can inspire us with words for such a quest and the acknowledgement of words suitable for it. Even if the latter must begin before finding these words, some words from the one or from the other can shed light on the path to be followed. It is through the unfolding of desire in search of 'to be' that a new word can arise, full of a meaning restored by the incarnation of the relational being of humans. Such incarnation can take place neither exclusively and originally in society, in particular the one that is henceforth governed by a scientific and technical power, nor in mere nature. It can be achieved by the union of living nature with the word of desire which arises in an amorous meeting between two humans who are naturally different.

No doubt, some people will laugh at the proposal to build the world on new foundations from the relationship of desire and love between us. I am afraid that their own projections regarding the future, supposing that they are still capable of having some, contribute only towards wasting the remainder of our living energy for the automation of a world in which people turn into robots—which amounts to the fabrication of monkey-like beings. In order to resist the increasing ascendency of scientific and technological power we can resort to our desire, in particular our amorous desire.

Already Plato asserted through the words of Phaedrus in the *Symposium* that 'if it would exist a means of forming a state and an army with lovers and their beloveds...it would be impossible, few though they are...that they do not win over the whole. As for Nietzsche, he teaches us in *Thus Spoke Zarathustra* (in the chapter The Stillest Hour) that 'Thoughts that come on dove's feet direct the world'.

Bibliography

Biemel, W. (2000 [1950]) *Le concept de monde chez Heidegger*. Paris/Louvain: Vrin.

Hegel, G.W.F. (2004 [1830]) Hegel's Philosophy of Nature: Part Two of The Encyclopedia of the Philosophical Sciences (1830). In *Phenomenology of Spirit*, A.V. Miller and J.N. Findlay (eds.). Oxford: Oxford University Press.

Heidegger, M. (1971) A Dialogue on Language Between a Japanese and an Inquirer. In *On the Way to Language*, pp. 1–54, transl. Peter D. Hertz. New York: Harper & Row.

Heidegger, M. (1971) *Poetry, Language, Thought*, transl. Albert Hofstadter. New York: Harper & Row.

Heidegger, M. (1982) *On the Way to Language*. New York: Harper & Row.

Heidegger, M. (1998 [1939]) On the Essence and Concept of Φύσισ in Aristotle's Physics B, 1. In William McNeill (ed.) *Pathmarks*, pp. 183–230. Cambridge: Cambridge University Press.

Heidegger, M. (2000 [1953]) *Introduction to Metaphysics*, transl. Gregory Fried and Richard Polt. New Haven, CT: Yale University Press.

Heidegger, M. (2008) *Basic Writings*, David F. Krell (ed.). New York: Harper & Row.

Husserl, E. (1973 [1900]) *Logical Investigations*, transl. J. N. Findlay. London: Routledge.

© The Author(s) 2017
L. Irigaray, *To Be Born*, DOI 10.1007/978-3-319-39222-6

Irigaray, L. (1994) *Je, tu, nous, Toward a Culture of Difference*, trans. Alison Martin. New York: Routledge.

Irigaray, L. (1996) *I Love to You*, trnas; Alison Martin. New York: Routledge.

Irigaray, L. (2004) *Luce Irigaray: Key Writings*. New York: Continuum.

Irigaray, L. (2016) *Through Vegetal Being, co-authored with Michael Marder*. New York, NY: Columbia University Press.

Irigaray, L. (Forthcoming). What the Vegetal World says to us. In *The Language of Plants*, coedited by Monica Gagliano, John Ryan and Patricia Vieira. Minneapolis: Minnesota Press.

Merleau-Ponty, M. (1968) *The Visible and the Invisible: Followed by Working Notes*, transl. Alphonso Lingis. Evanston, IL: Northwestern University Press.

Nietzsche, F. (2005 [1883]) *Thus Spoke Zarathustra*, transl. Graham Parkes. Oxford: Oxford University Press.

Plato. (1989). *The Symposium*, trans. Alexander Nehamas and Pay Woodruff. Indianapolis: Hackett Publishing Company.

Sartre, J.-P. (2001 [1943]) *Being and Nothingness: An Essay in Phenomenological Ontology*. New York: Citadel Press, pp. 413–433.

Tillich, P. (1952) *The Courage to Be*. New Haven, CT: Yale University Press.

Winnicott, D. (1953) Transitional Objects and Transitional Phenomena. *International Journal of Psychoanalysis*, 34: 89–97.